48 Laws of Spiritual Power

FRANK VIOLA

*Uncommon Wisdom
for Greater Ministry Impact*

48

LAWS
OF
SPIRITUAL
POWER

TYNDALE
MOMENTUM®

A Tyndale nonfiction imprint

Visit Tyndale online at tyndale.com.

Visit Tyndale Momentum online at tyndalemomentum.com.

Tyndale, Tyndale's quill logo, *Tyndale Momentum*, and the Tyndale Momentum logo are registered trademarks of Tyndale House Ministries. Tyndale Momentum is a nonfiction imprint of Tyndale House Publishers, Carol Stream, Illinois.

48 Laws of Spiritual Power: Uncommon Wisdom for Greater Ministry Impact

Designed by Faceout Studio, Spencer Fuller

Published in association with the literary agency of Daniel Literary Group, Brentwood, TN.

For information about special discounts for bulk purchases, please contact Tyndale House Publishers at csresponse@tyndale.com, or call 1-855-277-9400.

Library of Congress Cataloging-in-Publication Data

A catalog record for this book is available from the Library of Congress.

ISBN 978-1-4964-5226-9

Printed in the United States of America

28	27	26	25	24	23	22
7	6	5	4	3	2	1

To every person who dared to put their hand to
the plow of God's work—including those yet to be born.

CONTENTS

Effective Ministry and Spiritual Power

I wrote this book for two groups of people:

1) Those who regularly preach or teach God's Word. This includes pastors, teachers, missionaries, and church planters, both inside and outside the institutional church.[1]

2) All of God's people. Why? Because every true disciple of Jesus is called to be a servant—a minister—in some capacity. Paul reminded the new converts in Thessalonica that they had "turned to God from idols to *serve* the living and true God" (1 Thessalonians 1:9, NKJV, emphasis mine).

Every one of us who knows the Lord can have the glorious privilege of saying of Christ, "He is the One 'whose I am, and whom I serve'" (Acts 27:23, KJV).

If you are in Christ, your entire life is a "mission trip."

The word *minister* in the New Testament simply means "servant."

Paul of Tarsus took the concept a step further when he described his service to God using the term *bondservant* (Romans 1:1, NKJV).

Paul saw himself as a bondslave of Jesus Christ. His greatest boast was that he belonged to Christ and had the high honor of serving Him.

Unfortunately, many Christians today equate serving the Lord with church activities. But true service, according to the New Testament, is about advancing God's kingdom and destroying the works of the devil.

And these tasks require spiritual power.

1

I designed this book to set forth 48 laws of obtaining spiritual power for effective ministry.

As Paul put it in his most sublime letter,

> I also pray that you will understand the incredible greatness
> of God's power for us who believe him. This is the same
> mighty power that raised Christ from the dead and seated
> him in the place of honor at God's right hand in the
> heavenly realms.
>
> EPHESIANS 1:19-20, NLT

Spiritual power is another way of describing the dynamic energy of God. We could also call it God's "anointing."

Consider what happened when Samuel anointed David:

> So Samuel took the horn of oil and anointed him in the
> presence of his brothers, and from that day on the Spirit of
> the LORD came powerfully upon David.
>
> 1 SAMUEL 16:13

Consider also this passage from Isaiah:

> The Spirit of the Sovereign LORD is on me,
>   because the LORD has anointed me
>   to proclaim good news to the poor.
> He has sent me to bind up the brokenhearted,
>   to proclaim freedom for the captives
>   and release from darkness for the prisoners.
>
> ISAIAH 61:1

Jesus initially fulfilled this text when John baptized Him in the Jordan River and the Spirit of God came upon Him to launch His incredible ministry.[2] But the passage also applies to all who are in Christ and who continue His ministry today.[3]

The word *anointing*, therefore, isn't relegated to the Pentecostals or the charismatics. It's a term used throughout the Bible (Exodus 40:15; Leviticus 8:12; 1 John 2:27; Acts 10:38, etc.).

The Origin of the Laws

One of the most amazing truths in the universe is that God entrusts fallen human beings with His power. T. Austin-Sparks, a former pastor and one of the most Christ-centered and spiritually insightful men who ever lived, put it best when he wrote,

> God puts Himself into the hands of men. God is not going to move unless there are those who prevail with Him.[4]

Spiritual power—or God's anointing—can increase or decrease in a person's life.

Robert Greene's bestselling book *The 48 Laws of Power* inspired the title of this volume. Greene's book promotes the leveraging of human power through manipulation and selfishness. By contrast, this book promotes the leveraging of spiritual power through self-denial and the application of divine principles borne out in Scripture.

All the laws I explore either increase spiritual power in one's ministry or reduce it.

I've served the Lord for more than three decades, and I've discovered each of these "laws" either through my own mistakes (my rap sheet of mistakes is about as long as a telephone pole), by observing others put them into effect (for better or worse), or through my own personal labors in the Lord.

I gave an early (and clumsy) rough draft of this book to more than one hundred Christian leaders at an annual mastermind I facilitate.[5] The group included pastors, seminary professors, Bible teachers, missionaries, and church planters.

Most of these leaders said that the 48 laws were new to them, despite their theological training. Their encouraging words convinced me to professionally publish this book.

If you and I are to survive and thrive in ministry, we need to know about and apply the laws of God's work.

The Goal

My goal in writing this book is to encourage, inspire, and equip you for greater impact in God's kingdom. I hope, therefore, that you'll reflectively read each chapter with a heart open toward the Holy Spirit. As you do, I pray that He will speak to your heart and take you to new levels of ministry and beyond.

At the end of the book, I provide a web page that contains several never-before-released talks I delivered in pastors conferences and leadership trainings throughout the United States.

In these talks, I drill down on some of the 48 laws and add further observations about God's work.

I've intentionally kept each chapter short, distilling each law to its essence. Whenever I determined a particular law could use further illumination, I provided an illustration or story to demonstrate it in action.

The five codas at the end of the book are just as important as the chapters. (Coda means a concluding section.) If you go to 48Laws.net, you'll find several related audios and six more codas.

Two final words.

First, some laws may appear to contradict others, but this is a mark of their truthfulness. Biblical truth is often paradoxical. Jesus is fully God but also fully human. The Bible exhorts us to judge, yet it also tells us to judge not.[6] And consider these two proverbs that sit right next to each other:

Do not answer a fool according to his folly,
    or you yourself will be just like him.
Answer a fool according to his folly,
    or he will be wise in his own eyes.

PROVERBS 26:4-5

The laws of spiritual power often follow this paradoxical pattern. In some contexts, a law will apply one way, but in another context, it applies an opposite way. You'll see what I mean as you read.

The point: Aristotelian logic always breaks down in the light of God's eternal truth.

Second, I encourage you to supplement this work with two other resources. One is my landmark book, *Insurgence: Reclaiming the Gospel of the Kingdom*. The other is *Hang On, Let Go: What to Do When Your Dreams Are Shattered and Life Is Falling Apart*.

If you understand the gospel of the kingdom and embrace it, as I explain in *Insurgence*, you will find it easier to implement the 48 laws.

In addition, understand that, as a minister of Jesus Christ, you *will* go through some gut-grinding hardships. Some will be so horrific that they defy description. *Hang On, Let Go* will help you to be developed rather than destroyed by them.

Let's begin.

LAW 1

Never Hurt God's People

This first law is on a par with the Law and the Prophets. The cardinal law above all others is to never hurt God's people.

Before you nod in agreement, let me unravel what I mean.

Countless ministers have inflicted pain on the Lord's sheep while trying to advance their own ministries.

They not only defend themselves when under attack (perceived or real), but they seek to sever the heads of their detractors and "slaughter the villains."

Such fleshly reactions prove that they don't know the ways of God. (Perhaps they know them in their minds but not in their hearts.)

I refer not only to the obvious, like the pastor who robs his church blind and scandalously spends church money set aside for missions on extravagant personal expenses.

Hurting God's people is often more subtle.

I've known some incredibly gifted men in my life who have hurt the Lord's people in the following ways:

- Insulting individuals privately and publicly when they felt threatened by them.
- Outright lying to manipulate an outcome.
- Threatening people when they believed their reputation was at stake or they wanted to take full credit for something.

NEVER HURT GOD'S PEOPLE ∥ 7

- Masking hatred with sarcasm and ridicule with humor.
- Leveling false accusations against people in order to put them down and lift themselves up. (This is usually done out of jealousy or a spirit of competition. See 1 Samuel 18:1-16 for an example.)
- Mocking people out of envy.
- Demeaning those who make them feel insecure.
- Employing guilt, condemnation, fear, and/or shame to motivate God's people into doing something, even things believed to be right and good (more on this later).
- Correcting a believer in an ungracious way.
- Using people to advance their own ministries.

Such things wound the Lord's people at best or devastate them at worst. The result is a carnage-filled trail of damaged souls, lost friendships, broken relationships, and zero peers.

The Lost Art of Taking the High Road

Over the years, I've watched ministers engage in some of these tactics, resulting in massive wreckage. They leave people's lives in shambles, with no easy road back to healing.

Those who behave in these ways haven't learned to free themselves from their own self-sabotage.

By contrast, the Lord always calls His workers to take the high road, to repeatedly absorb the blows for the sake of God and His people. And most importantly, to hand their egos over to the cross (more on that later).

Consequently, like the Lord Jesus Himself, God's servants can endure injustice, mistreatment, and misuse without moving into the flesh and responding in kind.

They're also secure enough in themselves to not feel threatened by or jealous of other servants whom the Holy Spirit is using.

Put another way, God has called His stewards to put themselves in front of the train before sacrificing one of the Lord's sheep.

For this reason, Paul told Timothy that the Lord's servant must be kind to everyone, "patiently enduring evil" (2 Timothy 2:24, ESV).

That said, damage is sometimes inevitable. Some people will take offense, even if it's not your fault.

Still, hurting God's people is never an option.

It disheartens me to write this next sentence, but Christian leaders who have been sufficiently broken, who respond gently when criticized, who react with grace when corrected, who feel no jealousy toward others whom God has gifted, who don't feel threatened by those who have God's favor, and who refuse to return evil for evil are rarer than red diamonds.

Yet this is the standard to which the Lord has called each of us who serve Him.

The good news is that if you've hurt the Lord's people in the past, you have time to apologize to them and not repeat the same mistake.

In my early years in ministry, I made some boneheaded decisions that ended up hurting the Lord's people. Thankfully, I quickly apologized and made things right whenever I could.

Though some people will never accept your apology, the Lord will honor it if your apology is sincere and you've truly repented. And it's really His opinion that matters, anyway.

Scratch a Christian and Find Out What's Underneath

The most dangerous person on the planet is the one who will do anything to save his or her own work. But we have not so learned Christ.[1]

Most Christian leaders hurt God's people when they are attacked, criticized, or threatened, and they react in an ungodly way in order to "win."

I recall speaking at a conference with a group of other leaders. When the conference ended, some of us who ministered had lunch together.

One speaker, a well-known pastor, was livid. He began to describe to us a letter he had received from one of his congregants.

We could detect his smoldering anger as he rehearsed the letter, written by a woman who raised a legitimate concern.

She had tried to reach the pastor about an issue important to her, and it puzzled her why he didn't respond, despite her many attempts.

The pastor summarily dismissed her.

Instead of owning the problem, the pastor threw his chest out and told us how wrong this woman was for expecting him to respond to her. He bellowed, "I'm so tired of morons like this!"

Unhinged, he finally peeled off a letter to her. He laced his angry tirade with snide comments as part of his defense. He intended to "put her in her place" and justify himself as he did so.

He eviscerated her with his words.

This all proved one thing: Although this man could speak well in front of an audience, he knew nothing of the cross of Jesus Christ.

He knew nothing of brokenness.

He knew nothing of losing.

He reacted purely out of the flesh.

Equally sad, it appeared that none of his buddies saw this for what it was. None of them called him out on it. Instead, they quietly affirmed his fleshly reaction.

They, too, had been taught to castigate the opposition.

Here's the point: *The reality of your discipleship gets exposed whenever you get scratched.*

Those who truly walk in the Lord, not in pious rhetoric but in reality, can get scratched and not fire back.

They know how to absorb the hits and exhibit the Spirit of the Lamb in the face of criticism and persecution.

If this well-known pastor got in the flesh because a sister in Christ expressed her dismay that he didn't respond to her, then what would he do if someone attacked him unjustly or slandered him with malicious intent?

If racing against mere men makes you tired,
    how will you race against horses?
If you stumble and fall on open ground,
    what will you do in the thickets near
        the Jordan?

JEREMIAH 12:5, NLT

I don't think I have to answer that question.

I wish I could say that this was the only time I've seen this sort of thing.

I've watched famous Christians respond similarly—defensively and in the flesh—and I've thought, *How can they lead God's people while showing no signs of the cross in their lives?*

The cross is never easy to absorb. Not for you or for me.

When I first began serving the Lord in my midtwenties, at times I reacted in the flesh. I would get upset when I felt someone had treated me unjustly. I sometimes reacted with sarcasm when it would have been better to remain silent.

But the Lord used those mistakes to teach me the profound lesson to never, ever—under any condition—hurt God's people.

But to lose instead.

The Lord wasn't wasting His breath when He said,

Whoever does not take his cross and follow me is not worthy
of me. Whoever finds his life will lose it, and whoever loses
his life for my sake will find it.

MATTHEW 10:38-39, ESV

Herein lies a critical principle: When we lose, lay our lives down, and absorb mistreatment for Jesus' sake, then God gives His power to us.

Paul underlines this discovery when he describes the pain he endured from his "thorn in the flesh."

He [Jesus] said to me, "My grace is sufficient for you, for my power is made perfect in weakness." Therefore I will boast all the more gladly about my weaknesses, so that Christ's power may rest on me. That is why, for Christ's sake, I delight in weaknesses, in insults, in hardships, in persecutions, in difficulties. For when I am weak, then I am strong.

2 CORINTHIANS 12:9-10

I believe Paul's "thorn" was a man motivated by Satan who mounted a calculated assault on Paul's life and work.[2] But even if you disagree, the undisputed point is that God's power rests upon us when we are humbled.

So you, dear Christian leader, whether actual or aspiring, how do you react when someone scratches you?

Don't make the mistake of silencing your conscience or justifying yourself. We all make mistakes. We all blow it from time to time.

But if you automatically react in the flesh and no instinct in you tells you that your reaction is carnal, then something is desperately wrong with your heart.

Here's a yardstick to evaluate your spiritual maturity: How do you react when threatened? And what do you do when under pressure?

I don't care how many followers you have on social media, how big your congregation is, or what big names you can drop. This question gets down to the naked reality of what you're made of.

Your reaction to criticism and pressure reveals more about your spiritual stature than all the glorious messages you've ever delivered, all the books you've ever signed, or all the "great" people you've taken selfies with.

Unfortunately, the air of brokenness is too rarified for many ministers to breathe today. So I exhort you: Stand apart and breathe it in.

Confront your own self-sabotage and never hurt God's people. Be willing to die instead.

Even if it means losing your work.

Do Not Be a People Pleaser

One of the most life-sucking elements in spiritual service is being a people pleaser.

This mindset and attitude, if not ruthlessly dealt with, will end up undermining your ministry and depleting you of spiritual power.

Being a people pleaser will attract damaged people into your life who will end up turning on you and creating havoc in your world.

People pleasers eventually find themselves perpetually defeated and discontented.

Why? Because they have allowed themselves to become slaves to mere mortals rather than to the living God. (You may want to run that sentence by again.)

Listen to these heart-searing words from Paul:

> For am I now seeking the approval of man, or of God? Or am I trying to please man? If I were still trying to please man, I would not be a servant of Christ.
> GALATIANS 1:10, ESV

Point: You can't serve Christ and seek to please humans.

You're Not Pizza

On one of my birthdays, a relative gave me a plaque that reads, "You can't make everyone happy. You're not pizza."

Those words ought to be chiseled on the hearts of all who serve God.

You're not pizza. You can't make everybody happy, and it's a profound mistake to try.

So why not quit while you're ahead (or behind)?

Jesus was kind, gracious, and compassionate, but He was never a people pleaser. He didn't always respond to the needs of mortals.

Instead, He was driven by the leading of His Father. And the two didn't always coincide. The sickness of Lazarus is a case in point.

If Jesus were a people pleaser, He would have dropped everything as soon as Mary and Martha sent Him their desperate plea to visit Bethany when Lazarus became ill.

But Jesus delayed. Intentionally.

Why? Because His Father had other plans, and our Lord's sole ambition was to please His Father rather than us mortals.

The Lord always knows what's needed, and He's always on time. He just doesn't utilize our calculations or yardsticks. In fact, He lives in a completely different time zone.

The Root Behind People Pleasing

Christian leaders often have a penchant to please people. But it's really a symptom of a deeper issue.

People pleasing usually stems from a deficient sense of self-worth. Men and women seek to please others because they want to be accepted and loved.

Very often, people pleasers experienced poor treatment in their childhood. So at some point they subconsciously concluded that in order to be treated well, they must make others happy.

Here are some prominent signs that you are engaging in people pleasing:

- You hide your real opinions and outwardly agree with others.
- You over-apologize, even for things that aren't your fault.
- You feel responsible for how others feel.

- You find it almost impossible to say "no" when you're asked for something.
- You need people to praise you to feel relaxed and content.
- You abandon your personal values to avoid conflict.

The Antidote to People Pleasing

The antidote for the disease of people pleasing is to have your own Gethsemane with fear—the fear of man.

> Fear of man will prove to be a snare,
>   but whoever trusts in the LORD is kept safe.
>
> PROVERBS 29:25

If you fear God, you don't have to fear anything else.

> Don't let people call you a traitor for staying true to God.
> Don't you panic as so many of your neighbors are doing
> when they think of Syria and Israel attacking you. Don't fear
> anything except the Lord of the armies of heaven! If you fear
> him, you need fear nothing else.
>
> ISAIAH 8:12-13, TLB

I define the fear of God the same way that A. W. Tozer defined reverence: "the astonished awe that comes to the human heart when God is seen."[1]

Decide now to switch your allegiance from pleasing others to pleasing God.

In 1 Thessalonians 2:3-12, Paul described his own ministry mind-set. These were the marks of his ministry to God's people:

- He had pure motives.
- He didn't attempt to deceive.
- He felt confident in God's approval of him as a man entrusted with the gospel.
- He sought to please God, not men.

- He recognized that God tested his heart.
- He didn't use flattery or embrace greed.
- He didn't seek glory from people.
- He didn't exercise his authority as an apostolic worker.
- He shared himself, not just the gospel, with the believing communities.
- He paid his own way so that he wasn't a burden on any church or individual.
- He conducted himself in a holy, righteous, and blameless manner.
- Like a mother caring for her children, he was gentle and affectionate toward the believers.
- Like a father, he exhorted, encouraged, and charged the believers to walk worthy of God.

You'll never get far in the kingdom of God if you constantly seek to make people happy.

Pilate, the man who had Jesus crucified, did so to "satisfy the crowd" (Mark 15:11-15, ESV). Don't make the mistake of walking in his footsteps.

Here's a simple assignment:

- Make a list of your core values. Then make a ruthless commitment to never violate them, no matter the cost.[2]
- Begin practicing the art of saying "no" with grace. A simple "I'd like to, but I'm just not able to swing it right now" or "I have a previous commitment, so I'm unable to" will suffice.

It can't hurt to post the following three verses somewhere you will see them daily as a reminder:

Work willingly at whatever you do, as though you were working for the Lord rather than for people.

COLOSSIANS 3:23, NLT

Serve wholeheartedly, as if you were serving the Lord, not
people.
EPHESIANS 6:7

So whether you eat or drink or whatever you do, do it all for
the glory of God.
1 CORINTHIANS 10:31

Responding to every need brought to you leads to ministry burnout, compromise, and depression—and eventually, blistering defeat.

Therefore, stop making decisions based on the needs, requests,
desires, and appeals of human beings.

Instead, discover what, when, and where the Holy Spirit is leading you.

And then perhaps you, too, may see "the glory of God" (John
11:4, ESV).

In short, you'll never reach the goals God has given you if you try
to be all things to everyone. You'll also lose spiritual power.

So don't be a people pleaser.

Beware the Empty House

Jesus once told the following parable about the perils of having an empty house:

> When an impure spirit comes out of a person, it goes
> through arid places seeking rest and does not find it. Then
> it says, "I will return to the house I left." When it arrives, it
> finds the house unoccupied, swept clean and put in order.
> Then it goes and takes with it seven other spirits more
> wicked than itself, and they go in and live there. And the
> final condition of that person is worse than the first. That
> is how it will be with this wicked generation.
> MATTHEW 12:43-45

This strange story applies just as much to today as it did to "the wicked generation" to whom Jesus first spoke it.

Jesus told the parable after the leaven-dispensing Pharisees accused Him of casting out demons by the power of Satan (Matthew 12:24).

Regrettably, today we have "grandchildren" of the Pharisees who continue to walk in the same footsteps, relegating anything they don't understand to the works of hell.

But laying that deplorable accusation aside, the parable contains a frightening truth.

Let's go back to Century One and meet a Pharisee who as a teen had a genuine touch from the living God. We'll call him Doron. That divine touch led Doron to reform his life. He "cleaned up his house," if you will. He eliminated the negative things in his conduct and put his house in order.

But there was a problem.

Doron didn't fill his house with the things of God. Though his house was well ordered, it remained vacant.

The result? The demon who originally left Doron's home found seven others—the biblical number of completion—and they all came to live in his house. As the years rolled on, Doron found himself standing in Jerusalem, leading a throng of thunderous cries exclaiming, "Crucify Him!"

And his end state was far worse than before he had any contact with God.

In effect, Doron ended up crucifying the very One he pledged his life to as a teen.

Even though his life looked outwardly in order, he was empty and barren on the inside. And he unwittingly became the tool of God's enemy.

Applying the Principle

The principle holds true today.

Sometime in the past, you met the living God. You knew glory and you put your house in order.

The years have passed, and you're doing all the same religious things you did before. But your house is empty.

If you leave the house empty long enough, you'll find yourself in a state worse than before you responded to God's call.

The parable teaches us that when we clean up our lives and put our houses in order, it's critical that we have a steady influx of God's life coming into our hearts.

Without that, we're ripe to not only backslide but to devolve into something darker than anything we were before we met Jesus.

A related point: You are the most vulnerable to temptation after you have ministered under God's anointing.

Why? Because the exhilarating power of God has just spent you. You've preached your heart out and you feel exhausted on every level.

For this reason, the most vulnerable you'll ever be to caving to your carnal urges is right after God has mightily used you in power. You are more susceptible to sinning then than at any other time in your life because so much has issued forth from you.

Behold, there's an empty room in your house! A void. And now you're extremely vulnerable, wide open to temptations.

This is why I recommend that those who have ministered under God's power do something satisfying and enjoyable—but appropriate—right afterwards.

For some, it could be a hearty meal with dessert (I prefer a steak dinner with a milkshake).

For others, it could be engaging in a pastime or hobby.

A person constantly interacting with spiritual things needs time to recuperate.

God made us body and soul, not just spirit. Consequently, each part of our anatomy needs time for rest, recreation, and recharge—*especially* after we've labored under the power of the Spirit.

So after God has used you, it's time to refuel. It's vital to keep all rooms in your house full.

The Tragic Littering of History

Have you ever seen a Christian leader not just revert back to the world but become worse than before he was saved?

I've lost count of such cases.

Similarly, have you ever witnessed someone operating in God's power in astonishing ways, only to be exposed as having a secret life of continual sin?

I'm a student of the passing parade of history, and in my studied judgment, what happened in these cases can be explained by the parable of the empty house.

These leaders had an inner reformation at one point in their lives, but they lacked a consistent inflow of spiritual life.

History is littered with examples of servants of God who fell into drastic temptations that shipwrecked their ministries.

In most cases, such temptations came right after God used them mightily in conferences, meetings, and revivals. It might sound ironic, but it's a fact.

Why does this happen? How can it happen? It happens because their house became empty, and they didn't fill it.

Recognizing this truth is the first half of winning the battle. The second half is to be quick to fill your empty house with good things.

It's profoundly dangerous to have an empty house!

Set your intention on refilling your inward parts with a regular influx of spiritual life.[1] After you have ministered, do something enjoyable and satisfying but appropriate.

Your inner home will eventually get filled with something, so never leave it empty for too long.

This is the path to sustained spiritual power.

LAW 4

It Takes One to Make One

This next law is etched in the fiber of the spheres. It's unwavering.

It can be summed up in one sentence: *It takes one to make one.*

Put another way, you can't give to people what you aren't yourself. And people will follow what you *are* more than what you *say*.

Consequently, if you want the husbands to whom you minister to lay down their lives for their wives, then you've just volunteered to lay down *your* life for *your* wife.

If you want to see the women in your fellowship avoid becoming gossips, then you must avoid being a gossip.

If you want the people you teach to be gentle, generous, and not cave in to worry, anxiety, or anger, then you must be that type of person.

If you want to see your fellowship pray more, share Christ more, and read Scripture more, then you have just volunteered yourself to pray more, share Christ more, and read Scripture more.

If you want to see the people to whom you minister be less harsh and judgmental, then you must do likewise.

Many of God's people suffer from guilt and shame. Thinking, *I'm not doing enough* is guilt. Thinking, *I am not enough* is shame.

Sadly, many Christian leaders struggle with these twin enemies too. (Thankfully, there's an antidote for it.)[1]

Do you want to see the people to whom you minister freed from guilt and shame? If so, then you yourself must be free from both.

Unfortunately, many ministers have been criticized so often that

21

they've internalized this negative narrative, coming to believe they are inherently deficient.

I've met pastors who've heard so much moaning and bellyaching about their preaching and leadership style that they came dangerously close to putting their heads in an oven.

In this light, the greatest ingredient to your impact as a servant of God is your own transformation. This includes refusing to embrace false negative words.

The idea that the key ingredient to effective ministry is personal transformation smacks in the face of virtually all pastors seminars and leadership conferences, where the emphasis is put on strategies, techniques, higher education, style, etc.

I'm sorry, but all that pales in comparison to your own transformation.

Why? Because you will produce in others what you *are* rather than what you *teach*.

The Greatest Hindrance

In his marvelous book *The Release of the Spirit*, Watchman Nee writes,

> Anyone who serves God will discover sooner or later that the great hindrance to his work is not others, but himself.[2]

The Lord's worker is always more important than the work. This is because you can't separate the worker from his work. The work will always bear the imprint of the person responsible for it—for better or worse.

Consequently, the worker's spiritual condition will always influence his or her work.

Arrogant workers produce arrogant people.

Leaders with the tongues of sailors will produce people who use profanity.

Backstabbers will produce people who backstab others.

Someone who lies like a pile carpet will produce disingenuous people.

Harsh, critical, and judgmental leaders produce people just like them.

Experienced marketers tell us that successful entrepreneurs spend 80 percent of their time promoting their existing products and 20 percent creating new ones.

If you wish to be effective as a minister of Christ, spend at least 80 percent of your time working on your own transformation—which includes getting to know your Lord and becoming more like Him— and 20 percent of your time improving as a speaker, leader, church builder, or administrator.

A man can take others only as far as he himself has gone. And whatever you are is what the people to whom you minister will be.

A related point: Never send your troops anywhere you yourself haven't gone. The first guy through the wall gets bloody. That's the price of leadership.

It takes one to make one. This is a paramount law—a principle of the universe.

LAW 5

Detest Celebritism

Fasten your seat belt. This chapter is going to be bumpy.

Longtime readers of my work know that one of the dead horses I've beaten over the years involves the celebrity culture in the Christian world.

Jesus once made a sobering statement to the religious leaders of His day:

> I do not accept glory from human beings, but I know you. I know that you do not have the love of God in your hearts. I have come in my Father's name, and you do not accept me; but if someone else comes in his own name, you will accept him. How can you believe since you accept glory from one another but do not seek the glory that comes from the only God?
>
> JOHN 5:41-44

A major obstacle to faith is the desire to receive glory from mere mortals instead of from the living God.

Those who lead in spiritual things are especially vulnerable. In this regard, history repeats itself.

> Yet at the same time many even among the leaders believed in him. But because of the Pharisees they would not openly acknowledge their faith for fear they would be put out of the

synagogue; for they loved human praise more than praise
from God.

JOHN 12:42-43

Perhaps the greatest way to shipwreck your faith is to embrace the
celebrity culture that dominates the contemporary Christian world.
This culture—which is a spiritual plague—encourages God's people
to treat Christian leaders like royalty.

The Saga of the Celebrity Preacher

We've all read the stories. A young pastor burns the midnight oil trying to climb the ranks. Ambition drives him like a presidential candidate with a thyroid problem. Eventually, he's not so young anymore,
but he's still trendy and ultrastylish.

He's fulfilled his dream. He's made it to the top of the evangelical
food chain.

Coupled with his meteoric rise to fame, his church has grown so
large that people queue up in long lines snaking around the building
just to grab a seat. He gets chauffeured to the rear entrance of the
church building before services and walks straight into a private eleva-
tor that takes him into the greenroom.

The first few rows in the auditorium are reserved for VIP members
and celebrities.

Skinny jeans and some of the loudest shirts known to mankind
make up his clerical uniform. They are accented by his obscenely
high-priced sneakers.

He strides to the pulpit accompanied by strobe lights. Stage smoke
fills the pews. The audience is mesmerized, just as it would be at a rock
concert (minus the cannabis).

When he's finished his onstage performance (delivering his "sermon"), the pastor disappears, never interacting with a single soul in
the congregation.

He has bodyguards (sometimes referred to as "armor-bearers"). He
also has a fan club, and his wife is called "the first lady."

Starry-eyed fans gawk at his family from a distance. People would give an arm to take a selfie with him. Hardcore fans imitate his dress *and even his accent*. (Gag me with a rusty soup ladle!)

He's achieved "stardom" in a man-created hierarchy of style, slickness, flash, and coolness. He has his own brand and no longer feels content to live without the prefix *mega*.

The celebrity pastor is both the salesman and the product.

Then, one day, the spiritual shallowness beating in his breast floats to the surface for all to see. His soaring career suddenly deflates as all the helium escapes, and he implodes.

But the show must go on (which is one of the two laws of show business; the other is to never let the audience see what you really are).

So someone else takes his place.

Regrettably, the path of this young pastor is not uncommon today.

The kingdom of God has no shortage of preachers and teachers with Babylon seeping from their skinny jeans and u-neck T-shirts. (All throughout Scripture, Babylon represents the religious system, which is part of the world system.)

At its core, Babylon is mortal man trying to reach the heavens to make a name for himself—and using bricks to do it (God creates stone; humans make brick).[1]

The Marks of Celebritism

The two outstanding marks of a celebrity are superficiality and inaccessibility. But God has no place for celebritism in His kingdom.

If you have no interest in the depths of Christ, you're wide open to be captured by celebrity culture. It thrives on shallowness and is fueled by ego and ambition.

Allow me to get practical.

If no one has a way of reaching you, you've elevated yourself to celebrity status. Regardless of how popular you imagine yourself to be, you can always set up a website, a blog, or a Facebook page through which people can contact you.

Granted, not every email or letter requires a reply. And if the load becomes too much, you can enlist the help of a virtual assistant or secretary to field common questions. Beyond that, you can create an FAQ page to cut down the volume.[2]

Yet there still needs to exist *some* avenue, even if only one, by which others can reach you personally.

Especially your peers.

When some leaders read my railings against celebritism, they respond, "But, Frank, you don't know how much mail I'd get if I were accessible." That being interpreted means, "I'm too popular to be contacted."

Hey, pinch yourself, dude. You're no Will Smith or Taylor Swift. I get tons of mail myself, so I know it can be managed.

Take a few steps down from that ivory tower, would you?

Your Lord remained accessible, even though His disciples didn't always get that. ("Stop bothering the Master!" they said. Yet Jesus would have none of it.)[3]

Are you more popular than your Lord?

The Corinthian culture was preoccupied with image, status, power, and self-glorification.

Paul resisted all these pitfalls, knowing that God's power is magnified and displayed through human weakness (see 2 Corinthians 11–12).

François Fénelon put the matter this way:

It is not at all surprising that you have a sort of jealous ambition to advance in the spiritual life, and to be intimate with persons of distinction who are pious. Such things are by nature very flattering to our self-love, and it eagerly seeks them. . . . Our aim should be to die to the flattering delights of self-love, by becoming humble and in love with obscurity and contempt, and to have a single eye to God.[4]

Here's my personal prayer on this score:

Lord, in all that I am doing, in all that I've done, and in
all that I will do, I seek to bring glory to You alone. I want
others to take note of You, not of me. Cause them to be
stunned by Your awesomeness.

Two Sobering Texts

When I think of the peril of Christian celebritism in our time, two
passages come to mind.

Because we loved you so much, we were delighted to share
with you not only the gospel of God but our lives as well.
I THESSALONIANS 2:8

Paul and his co-workers not only shared the gospel with the
churches they founded; they shared their very lives with them.

If you have an international ministry, this is clearly impossible.
But it's absolutely possible with some in your local fellowship, even
in a large congregation.

Then there's this passage:

People were bringing little children to Jesus for him to place
his hands on them, but the disciples rebuked them. When
Jesus saw this, he was indignant. He said to them, "Let the
little children come to me, and do not hinder them, for the
kingdom of God belongs to such as these. Truly I tell you,
anyone who will not receive the kingdom of God like a little
child will never enter it."
MARK 10:13-15

Could it be that the Lord feels equally indignant when contemporary ministers have handlers who keep the "poor, miserable laymen"
away from them?

Ahem.

Follow instead in the steps of John the Baptist and develop an aversion to celebritism.

> He must increase, but I must decrease.
>
> JOHN 3:30, ESV

It's no accident that the Psalmist turns the glory away from himself twice in this wonderful refrain:

> Not to us, LORD, not to us
>   but to your name be the glory,
>   because of your love and faithfulness.
>
> PSALM 115:1

Still more sobering, I wonder how many Christian celebrity leaders are truly chosen by God? T. Austin-Sparks writes,

> Another general thing about leaders chosen by God is that they, while being human, are in many respects in a class by themselves. They are pioneers, and pioneers are lonely people in more respects than one. In some ways they are difficult people. Their standard and measure has to be ahead of others, and as human nature generally likes not to be disturbed but would seek the easy way, the pioneer is often a bit too much for people. He is restless, never satisfied, always pressing and urging forward. The keynote of his life is "Let us go on." His is not the easy way, and because human nature does want the easy way the leader is not always popular. The whole nature of man is either downward or to a quiet and happy mean and smugness. The pioneer is therefore not always appreciated, but often very much otherwise. He is so much contrary to this mediocre gravitation. A part of the price of leadership is loneliness.[5]

The above thoughts are good medicine for anyone poisoned by the disease of Christian celebritism. So detest it at all costs.

LAW 6

Avoid Burnout

Jethro, the father-in-law of Moses, spoke these valuable words to Moses:

> What you are doing is not good. You and these people who come to you will only wear yourselves out. The work is too heavy for you; you cannot handle it alone.
>
> EXODUS 18:17-18

One of the greatest temptations for a spiritual leader is to be so consumed with God's work that you burn to a cinder.

In my early years of doing the Lord's work, I was a weekend warrior. I worked five days a week in the public sector, only to hop on a plane Friday, preach in another state for a weekend, fly back Sunday evening, and return to work Monday morning. It was a powerful recipe for burnout.

Eventually, I discovered that the Lord built Sabbath—rest—into His creation for a reason.

Jesus, who did more ministry than most humans, regularly retreated to decompress and recharge.

According to the Gospels, Jesus' retreats took on three different environments, or "landscapes of the sacred."[1]

First, He retreated near water: "Jesus withdrew with his disciples to the lake" (Mark 3:7).

Second, He retreated to a mountain: "And when He had sent them away, He departed to the mountain to pray" (Mark 6:46, NKJV).

Third, He retreated to a desert: "But Jesus often withdrew to the wilderness for prayer" (Luke 5:16, NLT).

The God of the universe built these three spaces into His creation to allow humans to restore, recharge, and renew themselves physically, mentally, emotionally, and spiritually.

But the trick is to intentionally find time to retreat. On this score, T. Austin-Sparks rightly said,

> God is more concerned with what is done in us than what we do for Him. He often reaches His end with us much better when we are in a state of inactivity than in times of much work.[2]

The Intention to Retreat

Since understanding this law, I've built regular times of retreat into my yearly schedule. Since I live in Florida, most of my retreats happen near water.

Though Paul said that bodily exercise profits little, it does profit. One of the ways physical exercise profits us is by increasing our energy—and energy is one of the major ingredients to our productivity.

Without productivity, your ministry will suffer loss. Here's a quick recipe for how to increase your energy:

1. Stay away from foods high on the glycemic index.
2. Avoid energy-depleting people.
3. Take Vitamin B supplements.
4. Drink a lot of water each day (at least 60 ounces).
5. Practice deep breathing.
6. Listen to music that you find energizing.
7. Get sufficient sunlight (if you live in the North, consider SAD lights).
8. Take breaks throughout the day.

9. Find out what inspires you and regularly expose yourself to those things.
10. Build into your yearly schedule retreats, either near water, mountains, or deserts (or all of them).

It's vital that you periodically pump the brakes on your ministry and reset your spiritual CPU, rebooting it back to Jesus Christ.

Someone once said, "A candle loses nothing by lighting another candle." Though this may be true for candles, it's not true for ministry.

A better analogy for ministry is expending the battery life in your smartphone. The battery must be recharged for the phone to function. This is why Jesus often slipped away from the crowds to a desert, water, or a mountain in order to recharge.

He reset Himself in His Father's presence.

You can't burn the candle on both ends without eventually losing your health. Epaphroditus almost died because he never took a vacation from ministry (see Philippians 2:25-30),[3] and he's not the only such man in history.

When you grow tired, you stop giving as much. You don't love as much. You don't listen as well. And you stop paying attention.

So practice what every airline passenger is told before the plane leaves the runway: "Put on your oxygen mask first."

At first glance, this may appear selfish, but it's actually wise and loving. How can you help anyone else if you've stopped breathing?

The same is true in ministry.

Consequently, when the embers get low and you're running on fumes, stop running. Spiritual redlining isn't an option.

Stop. Rest. Recoup. Refuel. Reset.

You endanger everyone around you when you deplete your spiritual reserves without replenishing them.

Consider the following passage and take it as a personal invitation:

Then, because so many people were coming and going that
they did not even have a chance to eat, he said to them,

"Come with me by yourselves to a quiet place and get some
rest." So they went away by themselves in a boat to a solitary
place.

MARK 6:31-32

Never set yourself on fire to keep others warm. Give yourself an
off-ramp from time to time. Set your intention to withdraw to a solitary place regularly to recharge and reboot.

Don't burn out; keep yourselves fueled and aflame. Be alert
servants of the Master, cheerfully expectant. Don't quit in
hard times; pray all the harder.

ROMANS 12:11-12, MSG

Someone once said, "You can't burn out if you're not on fire."
Another said, "Don't rust out; burn out." Neil Young said (and Kurt
Cobain sadly repeated), "It's better to burn out than to fade away."[4]

But all of these are false choices. By employing the prescriptions in
this book, you can avoid rust-out, burnout, and fade-out.

Leave the Results with God

Ministers of God's Word often wonder how their words were received after they've preached or taught.

It's perfectly normal to want to know the kind of impact you've had. But most preachers, in my observation, concern themselves too much with it.

I'm sure you're familiar with these questions:

"Who was moved? Who was touched? Who was illuminated? Who was transformed? How many *really* turned to Jesus? Do I still have my fastball?"

But here's the thing: You will never know the full extent of your influence. So it's a mistake to fixate on it.

After you minister, simply rest and leave the results with God.

Though sometimes the Lord will give you a small peek into the fruit of your ministry, most of the time He will not.

The Oracles of God

Of course, I base all of this on the assumption that what you minister comes from the Lord. God has promised that when we proclaim His Word, it will not return void:

> So is my word that goes out from my mouth:
>   It will not return to me empty,
>   but will accomplish what I desire
>   and achieve the purpose for which I sent it.

ISAIAH 55:11

In this connection, consider two texts:

We have different gifts, according to the grace given to each of us. If your gift is prophesying, then prophesy in accordance with your faith.

ROMANS 12:6

If anyone speaks, they should do so as one who speaks the very words of God.

1 PETER 4:11

In the first text, Paul says that God gives us gifts by His grace, and when we prophesy (speak in the Lord's name), we do so according to the measure of faith that we have.

Peter echoes the point, saying that when we speak, we ought to speak "the very words of God."

The NKJV puts it this way: "If anyone speaks, let him speak as the oracles of God."

In other words, before you stand up to speak, it's vital that you have the confidence (the faith) that God has given you the message and He is enabling you to deliver it.

If you don't have such faith when you speak, then you're not ready for prime time. You may want to lay down your ministry for a while until you get clear on the specifics of God's calling on your life. (Has He called you to pastor, or preach, or teach, or something else?)

I've met many pastors who admitted privately that they weren't sure if God called them to pastor a church.

If you believe, "God may have dialed the wrong number if He called me to [fill in the blank]," that may be a good indication that you've misread your calling.

There's a big difference between those who are *sent* and those who *went*. Those who went don't have God's blessing.

Unfortunately, when someone feels called of God today, they are typically given only three options: Be a pastor, a missionary, or a music minister.

But the New Testament has a far more expansive view of ministry.[1]

Lacking the kind of faith for speaking that Peter describes could also mean you've neglected your first pursuit: knowing the Lord and hearing His voice.[2]

A Card That Made Me Weep

Years ago, before I spoke at an event, a young woman handed me a card. When my wife and I got to our hotel room, we opened and read it. The card brought tears to my eyes.

The young woman wrote that she had read my book *From Eternity to Here* a few years before.

One of the chapters saved her from suicide. She described how reading the book forever changed her life. She was "full of joy" because she could enjoy her life with her son.

After I read the card, I sensed the Lord saying to me that most people who have been impacted by my work in similar ways will never let me know. Even this young woman waited years before she told me what took place. If both of us hadn't attended that event, I probably would have never known.

At that same event, another speaker opened her talk by saying that when she had hit rock bottom several years earlier, she had searched the Internet for how God views women.

In her search, she stumbled upon my article "God's View of a Woman," and it changed her life.[3]

I had no idea.

Let me assure you that if you're serving the Lord by His power, you are impacting more people than you can imagine. But you'll never know the extent.

Your task is to be faithful. God's task is to handle the results.

Let Go of the Outcome

I've met too many ministers who exerted all their natural powers to engineer an outcome when things didn't appear to be "working" in their ministries. (I used to be one of them!)

Doug was one such individual.

Doug had a forceful personality. He was stubborn and over-confident in his opinions.

If you disagreed with him, Doug refused to let it go. The practice of "agreeing to disagree" sounded like blasphemy to him.

Doug lived by the philosophy, "We need to find the truth!" But for him, that meant, "I'm right, you're wrong, and I'll wear you down until you stop being a stubborn imbecile and yield."

For this reason, few people could get along with him.

When Doug felt that God had given him a "word" or some divinely inspired piece of advice for a fellow Christian, he would move heaven and earth to see that the person received it. If they didn't, he would push, prod, harangue, and even harass.

Doug had no qualms about frightening the gizzard out of people who didn't act the way he believed complied with God's will.

One of the mysteries of God's kingdom is that humans can resist it. Though the kingdom is available to all, it doesn't overtake or overcome anyone who refuses to receive it.

Jesus' exchange with the rich young ruler is a case study in how the Lord let go of outcomes.

Interestingly, we are told that Jesus had a special kind of affection for the young ruler. The Gospel tells us, "Jesus . . . loved him," which is an uncommon description.[4]

Jesus looked at him and loved him.

MARK 10:21

Perhaps the Lord foresaw that the young man would be called to become one of the seventy that He would later send out. Perhaps He felt that the young ruler was destined to become a pillar in the first ekklesia soon to be born in Jerusalem.

We don't know, but something special about this man drew unique affection from Jesus.

When the man resisted the Lord's challenge to sell all and follow

Him, Jesus didn't chase after him. He didn't try to persuade him about his misguided choice. He didn't badger him or try to terrify him into the kingdom.

Jesus let him go, trusting the outcome to His Father.

Two Bowlers

Imagine two men bowling with a group of friends.

The first bowler throws his bowling ball and watches it roll as it explodes into the pins. He then asks his friends what they thought about his technique. He's never bowled a 300, so he feels insecure about his method.

As soon as the second bowler throws his ball, he immediately turns around and walks toward the door of the bowling alley. He leaves the building and never looks back. He doesn't worry about how many pins he knocked down. He's perfectly content to have simply thrown the ball.

Whenever you minister God's Word, be like the second bowler.

Your mission is to live for the Lord and serve Him faithfully. The results are His domain.

Consider the following two texts. One is from Jesus, the other from Paul.

> He [Jesus] also said, "This is what the kingdom of God is like. A man scatters seed on the ground. Night and day, whether he sleeps or gets up, the seed sprouts and grows, though he does not know how. All by itself the soil produces grain—first the stalk, then the head, then the full kernel in the head. As soon as the grain is ripe, he puts the sickle to it, because the harvest has come."
> MARK 4:26-29

> I planted the seed, Apollos watered it, but God has been making it grow. So neither the one who plants nor the one who waters is anything, but only God, who makes things

grow. The one who plants and the one who waters have one purpose, and they will each be rewarded according to their own labor.

1 CORINTHIANS 3:6-8

In the first parable, all the farmer does is scatter seed. His task is then finished. The soil, "all by itself," yields the product of the seed.

In the second parable, God produces the results. Our task is simply to plant or water the seed. Both methods require patience. Seeds, even when planted in good soil, don't grow overnight.

As for that in the good soil, they are those who, hearing the word, hold it fast in an honest and good heart, and bear fruit with patience.

LUKE 8:15, ESV

The Aroma of Life or Death

If you are ministering Jesus Christ, your spoken words will carry the aroma of the Lord, something that can be detected beyond words.

That aroma will be death to some and life to others—it all depends on the hearts of your listeners. As Paul put it to the Corinthians,

But thanks be to God, who always leads us as captives in Christ's triumphal procession and uses us to spread the aroma of the knowledge of him everywhere. For we are to God the pleasing aroma of Christ among those who are being saved and those who are perishing. To the one we are an aroma that brings death; to the other, an aroma that brings life. And who is equal to such a task?

2 CORINTHIANS 2:14-16

When you preach or teach under God's anointing, the hearts of those listening can be opened or closed, receptive or hardened.[5] The impact of God's Word, then, is determined by two things: the quality of your ministry and the condition of the hearts of those who hear you.

One of my favorite stories is about a man who prepared long and hard for an important speech. After the speech, his wife called him and asked, "How did the speech go, honey?"

"Which one?" the man answered. "The one I spent three weeks preparing for? The one I actually delivered? Or the brilliant one I preached to myself on the way home?"

Are you focused on whether your speaking and/or writing impacts others? If so, give it up for Lent. Make your only concentration your own experience of what you teach and write. Then, quietly and confidently, leave the results of your ministry in God's good and loving hands.

Fully believe that your words will bear fruit. And trust Him with the outcome. He has promised that His Word will not return void (see Isaiah 55:11, NKJV).

This is another path to spiritual power.

LAW 8

Overcome Discouragement

As a minister of Jesus Christ, you cannot avoid discouragement. It's woven into the warp and woof of all authentic ministry.

I will shamelessly admit that I hold an Olympic record in discouragement.

If God has truly called you to labor in His kingdom, at times you will find yourself a spider's hair away from throwing in the towel.

You'll have days when you're hanging on by your fingernails and periods when you've completely dried out.

What kind of things discourage God's servants?

- You deliver a unique, stunning message under God's anointing on a topic that you've never heard anyone address. The jaws of many in the audience go slack. You hear from only one person afterward, who tells you, "I'm so excited! My pastor just preached on this same thing at our church last week. Thank you for the reminder!" Out of curiosity, you check out the pastor's sermon, and you're gobsmacked. His sermon was *nothing* like yours.

- You pour out your heart, trying to lead a backslidden person to Christ. Your words flow with the Spirit of God and the person appears visibly shaken. You pray for them, and they tell you they've repented and are turning over a new leaf. Two weeks later, they are back in the world, serving false gods just as they were before.

- You launch a new project that you feel confident God has led you to create. The first month, people favorably respond. But over the next two years, it grows at a snail's pace.

- You spend years discipling someone, investing tons of time, energy, and money to strengthen the person spiritually. He tells you and others more than once, "I'll never stop following Jesus, even if it means losing all my friends." Time passes and the individual chooses to make friends with unbelievers, who quickly corrupt him. You feel that all your ministry to this person has been in vain.

Any of those things ever happened to you?

Yeah, me neither.

Seriously, though, I've met countless ministers who felt so discouraged in ministry that the following self-dialogue often played out in their heads.

It's just not worth it. Should I just quit and try something else? But how do I quit? What could I do instead? Do I keep going? Then what? My goodness, make it stop! Where's my iPhone!?

Events like the ones listed above tempt many ministers to quit and take up fishing.

The Inevitability of Discouragement

On some days, ministry feels like lighting matches on a windy day while someone pours water over your shoulder.

Discouragement will come, but if it ever leads to despair, you're finished. You will have spiritually flatlined.

Discouragement is par for the course. Despair is spiritual suicide because it means you've lost hope. But being on the ropes isn't the same as bleeding out.

Read 2 Corinthians, and you will observe an apostle who fought the depths of discouragement. He even despaired for a time, and yet he survived. Listen to him:

For we do not want you to be unaware, brothers, of the affliction we experienced in Asia. For we were so utterly burdened beyond our strength that we despaired of life itself. Indeed, we felt that we had received the sentence of death. But that was to make us rely not on ourselves but on God who raises the dead. He delivered us from such a deadly peril, and he will deliver us. On him we have set our hope that he will deliver us again.

2 CORINTHIANS 1:8-10, ESV

Those of us who serve God must learn to joust with discouragement, or it will devolve into despair. And then the curtains close and we become another casualty of the ministry.

Fatigue, frustration, failure, fear, and loneliness all bring discouragement.

The good news is that discouragement is curable.

Elijah is not alone among the servants of God who felt like giving up because so few are willing to follow the Lord beyond the superficial.

The spiritual shallowness of our time, the lack of people who put more value on connection than "stuff," and the rarity of finding those who desire to co-labor with others can inflict tremendous discouragement on a servant of God.

David, the man after God's own heart (see 1 Samuel 13:14), had many first-class battles with discouragement. (Just read the Psalms.)

In 1 Samuel 30, we discover that David lost a major fight. As a result, enemies took captive his family as well as the wives and children of his men. David's soldiers felt so distressed that they considered stoning David.

Under the weight of all this, the Scripture says,

David was greatly distressed. . . . But David encouraged himself in the LORD his God.

1 SAMUEL 30:6, KJV

A Prescription

In *Hang On, Let Go*, I offered a practical prescription on how I've encouraged myself in the Lord over the years:

- Taking a walk and pouring my heart out to God.
- Listening to worship music and singing to the Lord through tears.
- Erupting in bitter weeping to God.
- Turning the Psalms about God's faithfulness into prayer.
- Repeating to myself various words of encouragement given to me by others.
- Reflecting on how God has taken care of me in the past and thanking Him for it.
- Reading some of my favorite authors who have written powerfully on the subject of suffering and faith. (In this regard, T. Austin-Sparks and Frank Laubach have been my closest companions.)[1]

In addition, I remind myself that I'm involved in God's work, not mine.

Consequently, if that which discourages me is going to change, the Lord is responsible for changing it. So I transfer the burden to His shoulders and come out from underneath it.

After a day or so, the discouragement usually dissipates. And God's anointing and strength begin to bubble up again, causing me to rise and continue.

Faith is unnerving. Risky, even, because it means we have to let go. But the sea parts only after we place our feet into the water.

Faith is seeing the future in the present, and it is faith that overcomes discouragement.

At the end of the day, realize that most of the obstacles that come your way in ministry are designed to be speed bumps, not flat tires. And your reaction will determine which they become.

> Let us not become weary in doing good, for at the proper
> time we will reap a harvest if we do not give up.
> GALATIANS 6:9

I'd be remiss if I did not mention something else.

The work of God is simply too painful and difficult if done without a genuine calling. The deep waters you'll pass through will be incalculable.

Continuing in a ministry to which God hasn't called you is a recipe for misery. It's simply not worth it to continue.

It *must* be a calling.

Yet you won't know if God has truly called you to His work until your ministry is on the chopping block, your work fails, and you get blamed for it.

If you can bounce back after staring death in the face, there's an excellent chance that you're a true worker in the Lord's kingdom.

The litmus test is this: Can you lose and fail and rise again?

Of course, God may be calling you to His work, just not to your current role. This has proven true for many institutional church pastors.[2] But that's another conversation.

LAW 9

Find Spiritual Satisfaction

I'm going to begin this chapter by making a startling statement: One of the greatest hindrances to loving God is serving God.

While that sentence may be difficult to grasp, it's true nevertheless.

Spiritual service becomes idol worship when we love ministry more than we love Jesus.

It's also possible for people in ministry to become spiritually bored.

As I've often said, everything wears out except for Jesus Christ. That includes spiritual disciplines, practices, activities, and service.

Even ministry that changes people's lives can become stale and routine, which is hazardous to your spiritual health. Remember, the boredom of God's people once produced a golden calf.[1]

Overcoming Spiritual Boredom

When people become bored and apathetic with their jobs, we call it "rusting out." The same happens when people get bored with spiritual activities. It leads to spiritual apathy and drudgery.

What breaks the back of spiritual boredom?

The answer: *variety*.

You break spiritual rust-out by seeking fresh ways to experience, enjoy, and encounter Christ.

Notice that I didn't say, "fresh ways of doing ministry." No, I said, "fresh ways to experience, enjoy, and encounter Christ."

This requires experimentation and a spirit of adventure and exploration.

Repeating the same spiritual activities in the same way will make you (and everyone else under your influence) tired and old.

I've had the misfortune of meeting many seasoned ministers who were still doing the same things they were doing thirty-plus years ago. Their spiritual passion had evaporated, leaving them listless. They simply went through the motions. No life or anointing blessed their activities.

They'd rusted out.

The antidote for this problem is to seek and find spiritual satisfaction.

Dallas Willard had some fantastic insights on this subject. Consider these gems:

Men and women in ministry who are not finding satisfaction in Christ are likely to demonstrate that with overexertion and overpreparation for speaking and with no peace about what they do after they do it. If we have not come to the place of resting in God, we will go back and think, *Oh, if I'd done this*, or *Oh, I didn't do that*. When you come to the place where you are drinking deeply from God and trusting him to act with you, there is peace about what you have communicated.[2]

All of your spiritual activities, no matter how outwardly impressive, are worthless if you're not continually being conformed to the image of your Lord and seeking fresh ways to be satisfied in Him.

Spiritual boredom has caused many women and men to destroy their ministries. Willard explains,

The preacher who does not minister in that satisfaction is on dangerous ground. . . . I know my temptations come out of situations where I am dissatisfied, not content. I am worried about something or not feeling the sufficiency I know is there. If I have a strong temptation, it will be out of my dissatisfaction.

The moral failures of ministers usually are over one of three things: sex, money or power. That always comes out of dissatisfaction. . . . The surest guarantee against failure is to be so at peace and satisfied with God that when wrongdoing presents itself, it isn't even interesting. That is how we stay out of temptation.[3]

When a spiritually satisfied person preaches or teaches, that satisfaction comes through. People can sense it. A peace, a rest, and a contentment stand behind the words.

There's also an authority, the same authority that impressed those who heard Jesus. Something intangible beyond His words seeped through (Matthew 7:29).

The Chief Pursuit

The practice of remaining silent in God's presence, doing nothing but beholding Him, is a lost art today.

And we all, with unveiled face, beholding the glory of the Lord, are being transformed into the same image from one degree of glory to another. For this comes from the Lord who is the Spirit.

2 CORINTHIANS 3:18, ESV

If we are to grow in the Spirit, it's vital that we learn to slow our minds down and put away all distractions in order to behold our Lord in quiet simplicity. Blaise Pascal's haunting observation is fitting:

I have discovered that all the unhappiness of men arises from one single fact, that they cannot stay quietly in their own chamber.[4]

In this regard, Willard offers some great advice on how to find satisfaction in the Lord:

I encourage [ministers] to have substantial times every
week when they do nothing but enjoy God. That may
mean walking by a stream, looking at a flower, listening
to music, or watching your children or grandchildren play
without your constantly trying to control them. Experience
the fullness of God, think about the good things God has
done for you, and realize he has done well by you. If there
is a problem doing that, then work through the problem,
because we cannot really serve him if we do not genuinely
love him.[5]

I'll add one practical point. *Experiment.* And when you're finished,
experiment some more.

Try many ways to encounter the Lord and approach Scripture,
then stick to what works. When that wears out, pick another approach
and stay with it.

Knowing the Lord is an adventure, so get out on that ocean and
sail it.

Elsewhere, I've provided a list of exercises to employ in this pursuit. If nothing else, they will give you a start.[6] But so long as you
find something that gives life and draws your heart closer to Christ,
keep at it.

As a minister of God's Word, your chief task is to know Jesus
Christ:

That I may know him, and the power of his resurrection,
and the fellowship of his sufferings, being made conformable
unto his death.

PHILIPPIANS 3:10, KJV

T. Austin-Sparks said it best when he wrote,

It is of the greatest importance for the Lord's children to
recognize fully that, above all other things, His object is that

they should know Him. This is the all-governing end of all
His dealings with us. This is the greatest of all our needs.[7]

Knowing Christ requires a steady, inexorable, intentional pursuit
of Him.

It also requires a rapacious desire to connect with Jesus, a desire
that must march on throughout your life.

Preaching and teaching are like taking a magnifying glass and
showing people how epic Jesus Christ really is. But in order to do
this, you must first find Him yourself.

You can't magnify what you don't see.

Too many preachers expect God's people to respond to their
appeals for more prayer, more love, more service, more patience, etc.,
when they themselves have a thin and superficial relationship with
the Lord.

Pursuing the Lord begins with a hunger and thirst to know Christ.
(I say "Christ" because God is known in and through Christ. Jesus is
God enfleshed.)

The Law and the Prophets hang on this one thing. Seek spiritual
satisfaction with passion and deliberation, and live out your days there.

Our ministry is an outflow of our pursuit of Christ. Without that,
it won't have staying power.

Ignore this law at your own peril.

Refuse to Take Offense

In *God's Favorite Place on Earth*, I spilled a lot of ink explaining what to do when other Christians hurt you. The theme of living without offense runs throughout the book.

In this chapter, I'll add to what I wrote there.

If you're in ministry, people will call you horrible things. Some of it will sting, so much so that you'll be tempted to retaliate. But if you want God to use you in power, you'll have to consistently refuse to take the bait. An important key to maintaining this kind of self-mastery and restraint is to understand the anatomy of an offense.

The Anatomy of an Offense

It doesn't matter how pristine your ministry may be, some people will take offense with you and your words. They did it with Jesus, they did it with Paul, and they'll do it with you, so don't kid yourself. If you're impacting God's kingdom, it *will* happen.

Unfortunately, Christians can be the ugliest and most vicious people on the planet. (This gets back to the virus of self-righteousness, which is in the drinking water of so much of contemporary evangelicalism.) I say this as an evangelical myself, though the term has become virtually meaningless in our time.[1]

Injury from other believers *will* come. It's inevitable. But you can choose whether to take offense.

You can decide to take the high road and let it go or descend into counterattacks.

As a servant of God, you can't afford the luxury of being offended.

I feel so strongly about this that I'll put it in a sentence: *The servant of God must be unoffendable.*

In a fallen world, offenses are unavoidable (Matthew 18:7). People will enter your life who will love you at first, only to hate you later. Some will insist on thinking the absolute worst of you. Others will become insanely jealous of your gifting and God's favor on your life.

I've watched too many Christian leaders take offense and begin bombing the offenders "with God on their side" (or so they thought).

If you have thin skin, you'll never make it in the Lord's work without creating carnage.

The attitude that many contemporary politicians adopt—touchy, oversensitive, take-no-prisoners, give-no-quarter—is contrary to the spirit of Christ.

It's a grotesque (and immature) impulse to go after those who have slighted you with hammer and chisel. Reacting to personal hurt with rancor and by vilifying others is rejecting the hand of the Crucified One.

Instead, whenever you encounter mistreatment at the hands of others, go to the Lord and say, "Lord, this has ultimately come from Your hand because you permitted it in Your sovereign providence. I accept it as such, and I won't let it get inside me."

Maintain your peace and calm at all costs. These traits provide the evidence that you have put your trust in God and that you view the matter from His perspective.

Will this approach keep you from feeling pain, hurt, or disappointment? No. But you can transfer the pain, hurt, and disappointment to the Lord in exchange for His peace.

But this requires that you get behind the eyes of God and remember that what is taking place didn't escape His notice. He's completely aware and fully available to you through it.

Blessed Are the Unoffended

When John the Baptist found himself alone in prison, he began to doubt that Jesus actually was the promised Messiah.

Whenever we are in a dark place, the Lord speaks the same piercing word to us as He did to John: "Blessed is the one who is not offended by me."[2]

You can add this statement to the end of that sentence: "especially when I allow others to come into your life and cause you pain."

Blessed is the one who is not offended by Me.

This is the forgotten beatitude.

John the Baptist served God all his life, utterly, totally, and without compromise. He denied himself at every front, never drinking wine, refusing to wear fine clothes, and forgoing delicious meals.

And what did he have to show for it? Imprisonment. And eventually beheading.

To make matters worse, when John was gripped with uncertainty, Jesus didn't even visit him in prison. Jesus "social distanced" from John instead, sending messengers to communicate with him.

The forgotten beatitude kicks in whenever God doesn't live up to our expectations.

But what sinful men mean for evil God always means for good where His children are concerned (Genesis 50:19-21; Romans 8:28).

So again, as a servant of the Lord, you can't afford to be offended. Most of us find this particularly challenging in a day when the toxic addiction to outrage is not only common but celebrated.

Outrage, however, is not a fruit of the Spirit. It's a product of the flesh.

God's true servants are unoffendable.

A person's wisdom yields patience;
  it is to one's glory to overlook an offense.
PROVERBS 19:11

That's the standard to which you and I are called, and it's a key to spiritual power.

LAW 11

Lower Your Expectations

You'd be wise to build your life on appreciation rather than expectation.

If you live from expectation, you'll experience constant frustration and even anger, because life has a predictable penchant for dashing our expectations.

If you live from appreciation, however, you'll highlight those things in your life that supply joy.

To bring this closer to home, don't expect too much from God's people. If you do, disappointment will surely follow.

When I was a young believer, I used to think, *Well, he's a Christian, so he'd never engage in backstabbing.*

Or, *She's a Christian, so she'd never intentionally lie about other believers or spread gossip.*

I was living in a dream world.

Sometimes I still have to remind myself about the profound damage the Fall has done to us all.

A Pacifist on Attack

Years ago, a self-proclaimed Christian pacifist began unjustly attacking one of my coauthors online. (Yes, you read that sentence correctly. A "pacifist" had chosen to attack another believer!)

This individual publicly pontificated about the evils of war, the wickedness of military retaliation, etc.

But when someone rubbed him the wrong way, he became verbally violent.

When I told my coauthor how much this surprised me, he replied, "Are you kidding? Very few Christians practice what they preach."

(I think he thought I was an idiot in search of my village.)

Sad.

If you are in ministry, lower your expectations.

Really low.

"Frank," you might say, "why so negative? Is what you're saying really necessary?"

Let me give you an exercise. Take out a notebook, either digital or traditional. Then read all the epistles in the New Testament with an eye to counting the problems the first Christians faced.

Make a bulleted list of those problems.

Keep in mind that when it came to God's work, Paul, who wrote the bulk of the epistles, built well (see 1 Corinthians 3).

Even so, he couldn't prevent the first-class bloodletting that took place in Corinth, Philippi, Galatia, Rome, etc.

As I've pointed out elsewhere, most of the New Testament (after Acts) is made up of letters written by apostolic workers to churches waist deep in yogurt. They all had big-league crises.

Thankfully, we have an infinitely patient Lord. With you, with me, and with all of His people. As A. W. Tozer said about Jesus, "He knows the worst about you and is the One who loves you the most."[1]

The Half-Hearted

No matter how powerful your work in the Lord may be, you will always have the uncommitted, the peripheral, and the half-hearted in your midst, along with the devoted and sold out.

Light attracts bugs, and there will always be those who stand on the periphery who want to warm their hands at the fire of those fully surrendered to Christ.

How do you deal with such people?

How do you move them from the periphery to the center?

If you find an answer to that question, call me collect from a pay phone (okay, I know those are exotically rare these days, but you get my point).

Allow me to sound as if I'm contradicting myself. On the one hand, we must lower our expectations; but on the other hand, we are to have confidence in God's people.

Paul (and the other New Testament writers) held both contradictory attitudes in tension.

On the one hand, they had profound confidence in God's people.[2] Paul trusted his ability to build with imperishable materials as he relied on God's power working through him.

Yet on the other hand, he didn't expect too much out of God's people, as he was well acquainted with the frailty of the human condition.

This is why he wasn't devastated when he found out that the Corinthians slept with prostitutes, got drunk at the Lord's Supper, took one another to court, fractured the church over their favorite apostle, and even denied the resurrection.

Read 1 Corinthians carefully and you'll never find Paul falling to pieces. On the contrary, he writes with grace and kindness, steadfastly reminding the Corinthians who they are in Christ and who Christ is in them.

Amazing!

On Giving Advice

I stopped giving unsolicited advice a long time ago. (There are some rare exceptions.)

I don't give unsolicited advice because people rarely receive it, and it often creates conflict. Over the years, I've discovered three facts about advice (which aren't unique to me):

- Those who need advice the most are the ones most apt to reject it.

- Whenever you give advice, be prepared to take responsibility for it, because some people may actually take it!
- In the words of one person, "Advice is like snow: the softer it falls, the deeper it goes."

In light of the above, it's always better to *connect* before you *correct*. To give *affirmation* before offering *advice*.

Consider how Jesus issues correction and advice in the book of Revelation. He first commends the churches before He drops the sledgehammer of rebuke and wields the surgeon's knife of godly advice.

Lower your expectations and never be quick to give advice.

LAW 12

Use Humor to Connect and Disarm

In *Jesus: A Theography*, my coauthor and I dedicate an entire section to the humor Jesus employed during His earthly ministry.[1]

We miss this element in the twenty-first century because we don't understand Hebrew idioms. The Lord had a great sense of humor, and He often used sharp irony to make a point.

If you're a minister of God's Word, don't take yourself too seriously. As Rick Warren once said, "Take God seriously, but don't take yourself seriously."[2]

Learn to laugh at yourself. After all, you're a joke. (If you don't think so, just ask your spouse or girlfriend/boyfriend.)

G. K. Chesterton rightly said,

Angels can fly because they can take themselves lightly. . . .
Seriousness is not a virtue. . . . It is easy to be heavy: hard to
be light. Satan fell by the force of gravity.[3]

One of the greatest needs in the world of ministry today is for those who serve God to develop a sense of humor.

Over the years, I've met Christian leaders who utterly lacked this element. They acted highly religious and intense.

They always looked like they were sucking on a lemon (or tightening their sphincters).

Such people were unbroken and dangerous, especially those who could sway audiences with their speaking gifts. (Not to mention that they're never the biggest hit at children's parties.)

Unbroken men and women are unhappy creatures. They possess no funny bone.

The antidote for this condition is to meet the cross of Jesus Christ head on.

The Potency of Humor

Humor connects people. It also displays our humanity.

In addition, it's an effective tool for disarming hot-boiling situations.

If you have an authentic ministry, you will face intense situations. More than once.

Many years ago, a group of pastors on another continent invited me to speak to them. Just before I arrived, I learned that the men wanted to bury my spiritual carcass. They intended to unsheathe their swords and liquidate me.

An older leader gave me a priceless piece of advice for the occasion. "When you are with these men," he said, "act as though you're about to fall asleep. Out-relax them. Take a nap if you have to. And never raise your voice."

I was keenly aware that I had hell to contend with that day.

When I walked into the room, it felt hotter than a firecracker.

Waiting for the daggers to appear, I slouched in my chair with a room full of thirty men who all sat upright in their seats, sporting intense expressions on their faces. I began to gently tease them and my interpreter (who was a friend) through humor and wit.

I peppered my teases with self-deprecating barbs.

Eventually, these men began to lighten up. After about fifteen minutes, they started to smile and laugh.

Though the pastors may have brought their fleshhooks, I never saw them. The Holy Spirit granted me the humor of Jesus Christ, through which I disarmed and connected with them.

Subsequently, I delivered perhaps some of the strongest words I've ever given to any group.

When I finished my message, the room froze. Clocks did not tick; lungs did not breathe. And I made it out of the building in one piece.

All of us realized that a tidal wave had swept through that room.

But it was through humor that I was able to relax the atmosphere and defuse the hand grenades as well as clear the air for a strong, uncompromising message.

This was God's grace, pure and simple. What took place exceeded my abilities.

I have zero doubt that if I had failed to inject humor into that meeting, I might not have survived to write this book. (Okay, I'm exaggerating. A little.)

Point: Learn to poke fun at yourself. Discover the art of the joke. Sharpen your wit.

Why? Because it connects, relaxes, and defuses, and in that respect, it can clear the way for God's power to be released.

Jesus was not a lemon-sucker. He overflowed with joy, and He knew how to employ satire, irony, wit, and humor. It's one of the things that made Him so compelling to the masses. And He is still the same today (Hebrews 13:8).

Don't take yourself too seriously. And never follow a man who always takes himself seriously.[4]

LAW 13

Be a Reservoir, Not a Canal

When we minister out of the overflow of an abundant spiritual life with Christ, we act like a reservoir. This relates to the concept of fruit bearing.

What is fruit, exactly?

Every fruit-bearing tree on the planet is a study in survival. A tree bears fruit out of the overabundance of life.

Each cell and fiber overflows with so much life that it must find a way to release some of that energy or risk drowning in its own vitality. Therefore, it produces pods on its tips and at the ends of its branches.

Fruit grows and drops to the earth due to the excess of the life contained within the tree.

Most often, whatever God shows us is first for ourselves to enjoy and experience and then to give away to others out of the overflow.

Bernard of Clairvaux described this law well when he wrote,

The man who is wise, therefore, will see his life as more like a reservoir than a canal. The canal simultaneously pours out what it receives; the reservoir retains the water till it is filled, then discharges the overflow without loss to itself. . . . Today there are many in the Church who act like canals, the reservoirs are far too rare. So urgent is the charity of those through whom the streams of heavenly doctrine flow to us,

that they want to pour it forth before they have been filled;
they are more ready to speak than to listen, impatient to
teach what they have not grasped, and full of presumption
to govern others while they know not how to govern
themselves.[1]

(By the way, never call him "St. Bernard." He's not a dog.)

Bernard teaches us to first be completely filled with the water of
life before discharging it to others. That's how a reservoir works.

People who function like canals have no time to be filled. Hurry is
their middle name. They never pause between the time God teaches
them something and when they share it with others.

Canals are always in a rush. They give out as soon as they receive.
They take no time to experience what they've discovered before they
dish it out.

Bernard continues,

The reservoir resembles the fountain that runs to form a
stream or spreads to form a pool only when its own waters
are brimming over. The reservoir is not ashamed to be
no more lavish than the spring that fills it. . . . When he
[Jesus] had first filled up the secret places, his teeming
mercies billowed over; they poured upon the earth and
drenched it, to multiply its riches. You must imitate this
process.[2]

I'll double-click on that last sentence: "You must imitate this
process."

Along this line, Paul told Timothy,

It is necessary for the hardworking farmer first to partake of
the fruits.

2 TIMOTHY 2:6, BLB

Charles Spurgeon wrote the following about this text,

> This is a law. No man has any right to be a partaker at
> all until he has first tasted of the fruits of the field. Until
> we have first tasted that the Lord is gracious, we cannot
> effectively or properly minister the things of God.[3]

Jesus Christ first filled Himself with His Father's living water before He dispensed it to others. During His preparation as a boy and later in an artisan's shop, He learned, discovered, observed, and was filled with His Father's wisdom. Then, at the right time, He began pouring out those riches to others.

Speaking in the same vein, Andrew Murray wrote,

> The first duty of a [minister] is humbly to ask of God that
> all that he wants done in his hearers should first be truly and
> fully done in himself.[4]

Preaching is like cooking. So taste test what you're preaching in your own life before you feed it to others.

Unfortunately, most ministers today don't do this.

Instead, they tend to ask themselves, "Will this preach?"

That impulse is stamped across the brains of most ministers today, but I want to challenge it.

When you find a dynamic book, article, or message, train yourself to respond with, "How can I experience this more fully?" instead of, "Where can I preach this?"

So many preachers and teachers come to Scripture with the mindset of, "Will this preach?" instead of with the mindset that says, "Lord, astound me with Yourself in these pages!"

Regrettably, few Christian leaders pray this way, and yet it's a secret to spiritual power.

Consequently, some unlearning is in order.

You'd do well to tattoo this on your eyelids: *You can't bring people into a living experience of something you haven't first experienced yourself.*

If it's not real in your own life, it won't have lasting impact in the lives of others. This is true even if you deliver your message with searing brilliance and soaring eloquence.

Mind Ahead of Heart

I began speaking publicly in my early twenties. Reflecting back on those days, I had no business speaking that young.

The reason is that I hadn't lived long enough, so my knowledge far exceeded my experience.

Those who heard me would often express appreciation and even benefit, but my messages had no lasting power.

People I led to the Lord eventually fell away. Even those who seemed to "get" what I taught quickly relapsed into old patterns.

Then the Lord put me in a series of unbearable circumstances where I felt desperate to experience Him firsthand. So I gave time for those spiritual treasures to take root in my own life before I passed them on to other people.

I let them marinate in the Crock-Pot of my own soul.

Through various trials and tribulations, the things I knew in my head dropped into my heart. Once the smoke cleared, I would speak, and I began to see the lives of my hearers transform. I said many of the same things I'd always said, but something else, something deeper and more powerful, started bleeding through the words.

I had learned the lesson of experiencing what I learned before preaching it.

This principle became a guiding light in my ministry and personal life. If I learn a truth about the Lord, but I haven't experienced it for a period of time, I wait to speak about it until I've proven it in my own life.

Personal Ambition

Personal ambition often prevents people from becoming reservoirs. Though the business world depends on ambition, it's toxic in the work of God.

God is the One who promotes (Psalm 75:6-7). As servants of the Lord, our only ambition is to know the Lord, please His heart, glorify His name, and remain faithful to our calling.

This is what the LORD says:

"Let not the wise boast of their wisdom
    or the strong boast of their strength
    or the rich boast of their riches,
but let the one who boasts boast about this:
    that they have the understanding to know me,
that I am the LORD, who exercises kindness,
    justice and righteousness on earth,
    for in these I delight,"
        declares the LORD.

JEREMIAH 9:23-24

How many people today are in ministry for power, popularity, and prestige? Many pastors are addicted to preaching sermons, hooked on making people laugh or cry. They depend on the applause.

But the only proper motive for our ministry is to show people the epic greatness of Christ.

So make *that* your sole focus and ambition.

Set your intention by telling yourself,

I exist for God's glory. I preach and teach to reveal the splendor of Christ. I don't want to try to impress people with my gifts or personality. I want to impress them—even astound them—with the beauty, majesty, and power of my Lord.

Burn those statements into the circuitry of your brain, because you will quickly forget them. By saying them before God, you will be setting your intention away from impressing people with yourself to impressing them with the Lord.

Be careful not to practice your righteousness in front of others to be seen by them. If you do, you will have no reward from your Father in heaven.

MATTHEW 6:1

When you speak publicly, forget about yourself.

If you're self-conscious, it's evidence of egotism. You're trying to impress somebody.

Lose face and speak to the needs of God's people, not the needs of your ego.

The servant of Christ who is well pleasing to the Lord does spiritual work in God's will, by God's power, and for God's glory.

Not that we are competent in ourselves to claim anything for ourselves, but our competence comes from God. He has made us competent as ministers of a new covenant.

2 CORINTHIANS 3:5-6

Like our Lord, our food is to do God's will (John 4:34). And we feed His sheep out of our love for the Shepherd (John 21:17).

Ministry as Worship

Any service that flows out of something other than love for Christ—which is another way of saying the worship of God—is in vain. On this point, A. W. Tozer has written,

What we are overlooking is that no one can be a worker who is not first a worshipper. Labor that does not spring out of worship is futile and can only be wood, hay and stubble in the day that shall try every man's works (see 1 Corinthians 3:11-15). It may be set down as an axiom that if we do not worship, we cannot work acceptably. . . . Fellowship with God leads straight to obedience and good works. That is the divine order, and it can never be reversed.[5]

I grew up in a Christian tribe where worship was restricted to closing your eyes, lifting your hands, and singing "praise and worship" songs led by a "worship team."

But the New Testament has a far broader concept of worship.

Worship is adoration and loving submission to the living God. It's the act of dwelling upon the goodness, greatness, and beauty of Christ.

According to Paul, offering our bodies as living sacrifices to God is "true and proper worship" (Romans 12:1).

Ask yourself, "Would I serve the Lord if no one ever noticed me and I never got paid for it?"

Hmmm . . .

Give this probing question some time to marinate in your heart before you answer.

One related observation. It's a common impulse for preachers to immediately consult the "experts" when reading a biblical text they don't understand. They scurry through multiple commentaries and online sources.

But I've found this advice from Tozer to be a much better practice.

A few minutes of earnest prayer will often give more light
than hours of reading the commentaries. The best rule is:
Go to God first about the meaning of any text. Then consult
the teachers. They may have a grain of wheat you had
overlooked.[6]

All told, learn to be a reservoir, not a canal.

LAW 14

Receive Correction

The voice of Jesus not only probes our actions; it also probes our attitudes and reactions.

And His voice often comes to us through other members of the body of Christ.

This is the great argument of 1 Corinthians 12.

Paul says that Jesus is not a dumb idol; He has the power of speech (verses 1-2). But where does He speak? He speaks through His body by the Holy Spirit (verses 3-4).

If you want God to use you in His work, He will deal ruthlessly with those areas of your life to which you're blind. Other members of the body who know you, however, can see them clearly.

If you are in the flesh, you will react when corrected.

If you are in the Spirit, you will act like a sponge, asking questions to understand what part of your life needs the penetrating light of God to expose and transform.

How a person responds when corrected reveals volumes about that individual's character.

When a little pressure is applied, it exposes who we really are.

The unbroken are quick to defend themselves at the slightest correction.

By contrast, a person who knows the cross will take all forms of correction to heart. They will exhibit a teachable spirit.

It doesn't break their jaw to admit that they are wrong, and they'll be quick to repent and apologize.

Long-lasting ministry comes out of being broken bread and poured-out wine. This principle is written in the stars.

Receiving correction and rebuke is painful. But the good news is that there is a resurrection on the other side of every cross.

However, you will not know the power of Christ's resurrection until you've first licked the wood of the cross and known the fellowship of His sufferings.

As I wrote elsewhere, "As high as God is going to elevate you is as deep as He digs to lay the foundation."[1]

How to Receive Correction

I'll put it bluntly: If you can't abide correction, you have no business being in God's work. You're a dangerous human being, dangerous to God's people and to unbelievers alike.

The effective servant of the Lord has strong opinions weakly held. He or she is completely open to correction on anything he or she believes or teaches.

> Not many of you should become teachers, my fellow
> believers, because you know that we who teach will be
> judged more strictly.
> JAMES 3:1

Humility is a first principle in the work of God. The ability to listen to correction without becoming defensive is its outstanding mark.

Here's what it looks like when believers receive correction in the spirit of Christ:

- They don't defend, justify, or rationalize.
- They ask questions to better understand the issue. (The person who listens the greatest is the most mature person in the room.)

- They are keenly aware that they may have blind spots.
- They don't reframe the correction as a personal attack (even when it is).
- They don't take it personally.
- They refuse to get offended.
- They don't impute evil motives to the hearts of those who are doing the correcting (they leave judgment to the Lord).
- They don't seek to lash out and destroy the reputations of those who did the correcting.
- They don't view themselves as victims but as students.[2]
- Even when the correction isn't accurate, they receive it as coming from God's hand. And they don't push back.

All of the above require the breaking of God in one's life. They are also a mark of those who are safe to God's people.

I Disagree with That

Years ago, I knew a young man who was engaged in ministry. We'll call him Joe. Like every young person (at age twenty-one, I was Exhibit A), Joe had innumerable rough edges in desperate need of transformation.

Joe was full of zeal. Bold but crass, he often hurt people. Joe was the classic bull in a china shop.

Through the years, many mature believers tried to gently correct Joe.

Joe's default response, beyond becoming defensive, was to say, "I disagree with that." He asked no questions. He provided no evidence of wanting to understand. He never hinted that he might actually be wrong. He displayed no humility whatsoever.

Before long, Joe crashed and burned.

I have no idea where he is today or what he's doing, but I hope he learned the critical lesson of being able to receive correction.

It's another law that cannot be ignored.

LAW 15

Distinguish Between Critics

If you are doing anything worthwhile for God's kingdom, you will invite fire.

Snakes get exposed whenever the grass gets cut. You will draw venom from some. And most of the time, they will be "religious" people—just as was the case in Jesus' day.

In fact, the more valuable your contribution to the kingdom, the more severe the criticism. (See Law 39 for the attacks leveled at Jesus and Paul.)

Perhaps you've heard the oft-repeated platitude, "If you're flying over the target, you're going to catch flak." Well, here's the opposite.

If you never want to face withering criticism, then preach nothing, write nothing, say nothing.

Ever.

Dogs don't bark at parked cars. And if you aim at nothing, you'll hit it every time.

Not all criticism is the same, however, so it's vital that you distinguish between critics.

As I've written previously on my *Beyond Evangelical* blog, there are three kinds of critics, and each one warrants a different response.[1]

1. **Supporters.** These people love you and support what you do. Any criticism they bring your way is constructive. It's designed to make you a better person.

    Supporters want you to succeed so they are cheering for you and your work.

For instance, if you're a writer, a supporter may point out a typographical or grammatical error. They may also draw your attention to a factual error.

Your Response to Supporters: Welcome their criticism because it's often priceless. These critics are doing you a great service by pointing out your blind spots and oversights. Always thank them for taking the time to draw your attention to such things. Sometimes it's not easy for them to do so.

2. **Objectors.** Objectors have a genuine disagreement with you. They aren't your enemy. Consequently, they aren't contentious or mean-spirited, and they don't misrepresent you or your work.

   They present coherent disagreements in a civil fashion. This makes them credible and worth hearing. None of us can claim immaculate perception. Therefore, be grateful for these people.

   Your Response to Objectors: Be open to the objectors because they may be right. Give them an ear and investigate what they say. It may turn out that they have an accurate objection, and they are doing you a service by correcting your thinking. On the other hand, by analyzing their arguments you may confirm your own position.

   I've found that when I have engaged an objector and we talked through the apparent disagreement, most of the time we discovered that we really didn't disagree.

   Martin Luther King, Jr. put it beautifully:

   > Seldom do I pause to answer criticism of my work and ideas. If I sought to answer all the criticisms that cross my desk, my secretaries would have little time for anything other than such correspondence in the course of the day, and I would have no time for constructive work. But since I feel that you are

men of genuine good will and that your criticisms
are sincerely set forth, I want to try to answer
your statements in what I hope will be patient and
reasonable terms.[2]

3. **Trolls.** Trolls are set on your destruction. Hatred, usually
rooted in jealousy, governs them. Trolls will first deliberately
misrepresent you. If that doesn't work, they will resort to personal attacks and character assassination.

Trolls are dishonest and traffic in manufacturing lies,
spinning the truth, and distorting facts. They often can be
described as "kooks," making ridiculous accusations and bogus
connections that are not only unsubstantiated but outrageous.

Trolls do not receive correction from anyone, so they rapidly lose credibility. Only the gullible and those who operate
by hatred support them. Trolls almost always attack people
they don't know personally.

Trolls repeatedly lift themselves up while tearing others
down. They are inflicted with inflated egos that have never
gone to the cross. For this reason, they are toxic to others and
are their own worst enemies.

Your Response to Trolls: All social media experts agree: Don't
feed the trolls; ignore them. If you engage a troll and try to
correct him or her, you will do so in vain. In fact, it's counter-
productive because it simply makes them appear credible and
draws attention to their dishonest statements.

A troll's behavior deserves to be treated with disdain. Trolls
do not dignify a response.

Since trolls are deliberately dishonest, there's no use in trying to correct them. In fact, to do so elevates them to a position they don't deserve.

Trolls are puny enemies. To engage or interact with them is
to make yourself puny and weak. Consign a troll to oblivion,
like an irritating gnat, by ignoring him or her.

Don't waste your time or energy getting entangled with a troll. Doing so will create a tar baby in your life. By acknowledging a troll's deplorable vitriol and despicable absurdities, you give his or her existence credibility.

As Proverbs 26:4 says, "Do not answer a fool according to his folly, or you yourself will be just like him." Eventually, trolls end up dying on their own swords. So give them no quarter.[3]

Each of the critics I've described can be Christians (trolls would be "professing" Christians, because they consistently violate Matthew 7:12 by their reprehensible behavior).

When it comes to criticism, it's important to remember that all things that come into your life—good or evil, complaints or praise—have first passed through God's loving hands before they got to you (Romans 8:28).

Receive constructive criticism with a spirit of gratefulness and ignore whatever is rooted in falsehood. Take the high road, as did your Lord when He came under attack (1 Peter 2:23).

Theodore Roosevelt spoke these fitting words about critics:

It is not the critic who counts; not the man who points out how the strong man stumbles, or where the doer of deeds could have done them better. The credit belongs to the man who is actually in the arena, whose face is marred by dust and sweat and blood; who strives valiantly; who errs, who comes short again and again, because there is no effort without error and shortcoming; but who does actually strive to do the deeds; who knows great enthusiasms, the great devotions; who spends himself in a worthy cause; who at the best knows in the end the triumph of high achievement, and who at the worst, if he fails, at least fails while daring greatly, so that his place shall never be with those cold and timid souls who know neither victory nor defeat.[4]

It is a test of your spiritual maturity to see how long you can go without taking offense when criticized.

Again, if you're ministering Christ, you will draw the reproaches of the intolerant.

Here's an exercise: Make a list of all your critics and identify each one's type. Then ask the Lord to give you wisdom in dealing with each of them.

LAW 16

Expect Misunderstandings

Many years ago, I gave a forty-four-minute talk on the Cave of Adullam as a metaphor of how Jesus Christ builds a kingdom community.

In my opening, I made a few brief remarks about psychology. I said that psychologists have discovered various stages in human development. The rest of the message had nothing to do with psychology, psychologists, or human development.

The entire talk focused on the developmental stages of an authentic church.[1]

When I finished the message, I opened the floor for questions. The first hand that shot up was from an older woman who didn't even ask a question. She made a statement.

The woman said, "You mentioned psychology. Psychologists disagree with each other; therefore, psychology cannot be proven and it's unscientific."

My first thought was that she deserved fifteen minutes in purgatory for making such an off-topic statement. Apparently the only thing she heard in my forty-four-minute talk on the Lord Jesus Christ and His body was my fleeting introductory comment about human development.

Welcome to the ministry, friends.

I have a simple point to make from that story. It's impossible to preach, teach, exhort, counsel, offer advice, write, etc., without being misunderstood.

Sometimes the blame for the misunderstanding can be laid at your feet. You didn't nuance your words enough. You weren't clear. You were sloppy and spoke carelessly. Or you had the audacity to use a word that begins with "psych."

Ahem.

At other times, the misunderstanding occurs because of a "filter" in the hearer.

In such cases, the persons listening (or reading) filter your words through the grid of their own experience. Either that or they missed the nuance, jumped to an inaccurate conclusion, or didn't listen (or read) carefully.

There are also times when certain words or images you use trigger a painful or sensitive memory for the hearer.

Straining at Gnats

I remember Jack Taylor telling the story of a preacher who once used the word *britches* in his sermon. (*Britches* is an old term for trousers or pants.)

When the preacher finished his talk, a woman said to him, "I'm offended that you used the word *britches* in your sermon! You should have used *trousers*."

The preacher replied, "Do you remember what I said before I used the word *britches*?"

"No," she answered.

"Do you remember what I said after I used the word *britches*?"

"No," she said.

"I see," he replied. "Well, I'm glad I used the word *britches*, because if I hadn't, you would have gotten nothing out of my sermon."

Of course, his sermon didn't focus on britches, pants, trousers, or psychologists.

Would you like a word of encouragement? People even misunderstood the flawless Son of God.

Jesus made a strange statement about how Peter would die. Peter then asked Jesus how John would die. The Lord gave a simple but direct response: "If I want him to remain alive until I return, what is that to you? You must follow me" (John 21:22).

The text then tells us that the disciples misunderstood the Lord's meaning and spawned a false rumor based on their faulty interpretation.

John recorded the incident:

> Then this saying went out among the brethren that this disciple [John] would not die. Yet Jesus did not say to him that he would not die, but, "If I will that he remain till I come, what is that to you?"
>
> JOHN 21:23, NKJV

We can gain two game-changing insights from this story.

The first has to do with Jesus' words to Peter: "If I want him [John] to remain alive until I return, what is that to you? You must follow me" (John 21:22).

These straightforward words inform us to never concern ourselves with God's dealings in the lives of others. We must focus on following the Lord ourselves.

Too often, we worry about what others are doing or not doing in their relationship with God. Or we worry about how God might be dealing with them. But Jesus gave Peter a sobering response to such worries: "How I deal with that person is My business, not yours. You focus on following Me!"[2]

In other words, don't worry about the responsibilities of others. Concern yourself only with your responsibility.

A game changer, for sure.

Usually, people apologize for something they've done while also laying blame on others. Example: "I'm sorry that I spit in your face, but you smirked at me, which provoked me to do it."

Okay, it's usually not that blatant, but it often comes close.

What does Jesus say about this? Something to the tune of, "You take responsibility for your part and don't concern yourself with the other person's part. Leave their part to Me."

The Perfect Communicator

We find the other game-changing insight in the second text. Jesus, who spoke perfectly, was misunderstood by His disciples. Read it again:

> Then this saying went out among the brethren that this disciple [John] would not die. Yet Jesus did not say to him that he would not die, but, "If I will that he remain till I come, what is that to you?"
>
> JOHN 21:23, NKJV

The disciples misunderstood the One who spoke flawlessly. So much so that a false rumor spread about what He said.

I remember reading this account many years ago when someone misunderstood and misrepresented one of my own teachings.

This both discouraged and perplexed me because I thought I had been crystal clear in my presentation. But this passage relieved and reassured me.

Even Jesus, the greatest communicator who ever breathed oxygen, was misunderstood by His closest followers.

Another game changer.

Since that time, these two texts have meant a great deal to me personally.

To sum up, on the one hand, do your dead-level best to avoid being misunderstood. Take pains to be as clear as possible. (There's one exception to this.)[3]

On the other hand, expect misunderstandings, because they will come.

Guard Against Self-Righteousness

There's a tremendous difference between righteousness, as the Bible describes it, and self-righteousness.

Self-righteousness is the pious, sanctimonious, smug, superior, and judgmental attitude toward others based on the warped idea that you are better and holier than they are. This religiously transmitted disease is contagious among "Christians." The only vaccine for it is a head-on collision with Jesus Christ, the incarnation of mercy and grace.

The Pharisees held PhDs in self-righteousness. This story from Jesus describes a self-righteous mindset and attitude:

> Then Jesus told this story to some who had great confidence in their own righteousness and scorned everyone else: "Two men went to the Temple to pray. One was a Pharisee, and the other was a despised tax collector. The Pharisee stood by himself and prayed this prayer: "I thank you, God, that I am not like other people—cheaters, sinners, adulterers. I'm certainly not like that tax collector! I fast twice a week, and I give you a tenth of my income."
> LUKE 18:9-12, NLT

In *Jesus: A Theography*, I put the problem like this:

> Something else made Jesus absolutely livid and was perhaps His greatest irritant: self-righteous judgmentalism. Survey

those to whom Jesus directed His strongest, most severe words. It was the self-righteous, judgmental Pharisees and Sadducees—those who didn't see themselves as sinners but who leveled that charge against everyone else. He characterized such people as "blind guides," "hypocrites," "fools," "whitewashed tombs," a "brood of vipers," and children of the devil. Not exactly kind words from a mild-mannered Messiah.

And to whom did Jesus show the most compassion? People who were involved in immorality of all types, such as prostitutes, adulterers, tax collectors, and thieves. It's easy for us today to acknowledge that Jesus treated the self-righteous more severely than the "real sinners" without applying this standard to our own context—or to ourselves.

But "Jesus Christ is the same yesterday, today, and forever." What He deemed to be the severest of all sins (self-righteousness) is what many contemporary Christians view as a mere misdemeanor. And the sorts of sins toward which Jesus had great compassion and patience are what many Christians place at the top of the totem pole of "serious sins," deeming them to be felonies. Don't be deceived: the "odious complacency of the self-consciously pious" is what infuriated our Lord the most.[1]

As a minister of God's Word, one of your most formidable enemies from which to guard your heart is self-righteousness.

There's only one Person in the universe who has the right to be self-righteous, and He isn't.

So take your cue from Jesus.

Pride goes before destruction,
    a haughty spirit before a fall.
PROVERBS 16:18

Therefore let anyone who thinks that he stands take heed lest he fall.

1 CORINTHIANS 10:12, ESV

Don't forget that the knowledge of good belongs to the same tree as the knowledge of evil. These two sides of the forbidden tree—good and evil—correspond to the two sides of the flesh.

One is the self-righteousness of the flesh (which flows out of the knowledge of good). The other is the defiling acts of the flesh (which flow out of the knowledge of evil).[2]

The tree of life differs completely. It contains divine life, which is *goodness* incarnate rather than mere *knowledge* of good.

Few things on God's green earth are worse than a priggish, supercilious, pedantic, self-righteous Christian. (But I can't think of any right now.)

A powerful prophylactic against self-righteousness is self-awareness, the sober consciousness that you are no better than any other Christian. And that you are just as susceptible to falling as they are.

I've watched numerous ministers fall into horrible predicaments because they were harsh in judging other ministers when they sinned or made a mistake.

The boomerang effect is built into the fabric of God's creation.

How can you tell if you have self-righteousness in your bloodstream? Simple. Pay attention to how you react when you hear news of another Christian leader failing or falling. If you don't think, *Oh dear, that could have been me*, then you're probably self-righteous.

This leads to the issue of correcting others.

How (Not) to Correct Another Believer

When I was a young Christian in my late teens, I was "rebuke-happy." I had no problem confronting and correcting the faults of others. The people I looked up to modeled this for me, and I benightedly followed their example.

I knew the Scriptures well, so I was cocked and loaded for bear with Bible verses in hand. I found some of my favorite texts in Proverbs, especially the ones that say wise people love reproof and fools hate it (e.g., Proverbs 9:8; 12:1; 13:1).

As I grew in the Lord, I came to some painful discoveries. One was that I had no idea how to correct another believer in the spirit of Jesus Christ. So I did more damage than good with my "corrections."

Another was that God didn't want me correcting everyone else, even when I spotted faults and flaws in others (which is nothing to boast about). The Lord didn't give me the job of adjusting the behavior of my brothers and sisters in Christ. I needed to pay more attention to my own spiritual walk than that of others (see James 4:11).

In my early years as a believer, I was part of a Christian tradition that was trigger-happy to straighten everyone else out. It was bad teaching that bred legalism and self-righteousness. And I was guilty of embracing it. I wish someone had taught me back then what correction looks like when done in Christ.

Here are fourteen things to consider before you correct another Christian:

1. *Never base your correction on secondhand information.* Don't critique what a person allegedly said or did; always go to the person directly to get the facts. Hearing one side of a story is a horrible basis upon which to correct someone. (I've been guilty of this in the past.)[3]

2. *Just because you see someone else's faults doesn't give you the right to point them out and correct them.* The ability to spot the flaws of another is no gift. If you begin riding that horse hard, your card will eventually get pulled.

   Scripture condemns fault-finding (Jude 1:16). And even non-Christian philosophers understand the evil of fault-finding. Kahlil Gibran has said, "Our worst fault is our preoccupation with the faults of others."[4]

3. *Many Christians have suffered significant damage because someone corrected them in a way contrary to that of Jesus Christ.*

4. *If you correct someone outside of grace, you will surely lose their friendship* (Proverbs 18:19).

5. *Your spiritual instincts will show you how to deal with an offense.* In Law 28 (Manage Conflict), I talk about three ways to manage a conflict. Let your instincts guide you on which best fits the occasion.

6. *Sometimes, Christians correct others when they shouldn't; other times, they let serious problems go unchecked without bringing needed correction.* Both mistakes can destroy others (see 1 Corinthians 5). It is virtually always wrong when someone hurts, oppresses, harasses, or misrepresents another. Ignoring such behavior is also wrong.

7. *If your brother or sister does something that makes you feel uncomfortable (rather than actually hurting you or someone else), then think thrice about correcting them.*

8. *When correcting someone, go to them in private, as Jesus taught us to do* ("between the two of you," Matthew 18:15). This also fulfills what Jesus taught us in Matthew 7:12: Treat others the same way you would want to be treated if you were standing in their shoes.

    Going to others (beyond the person you are correcting) about the problem is warranted only if the person has rejected the correction and keeps on sinning (Matthew 18:16-17) or if they are sinning against others in a public way. If someone misrepresents another person in a public forum, for example, then the person spreading the misinformation ought to be corrected in that same public forum.

9. *Ask yourself some questions before you correct another believer:* Is it my place to correct this person? Do I have a personal

relationship with them? Or am I being a busybody in another person's affairs (1 Peter 4:15; 1 Timothy 5:13)?

Have I borne patiently with this problem for a long time? Has long-suffering run its course?

Am I reacting out of pride, anger, or some other dark motive?

Have I agonized before the Lord, asking Him to remove the dark parts from me before I talk to my sister or brother?

Has the Lord extracted the spirit of self-righteousness and cruelty from my heart?

Have I prayed for this person, asking God to correct them first?

Have I gone to the cross before pulling the trigger of correction?

And perhaps most important: How would I want to be corrected if I were in this person's shoes?

If you cannot answer these questions with a "yes," then you're not yet qualified to correct your brother or sister.

10. *Be keenly aware that you are just as fallen and deserving of judgment as the person you are correcting.* The sin of self-righteousness is the result of regarding some sins (those of others) as being more serious than other sins (our own).

Remember, Jesus equated anger with murder and lust with adultery (Matthew 5:21-22, 27-28), and James said that if you break one point of the law, you're guilty of breaking every law (James 2:10). That puts all of us on the same needy level!

Be careful not to fall into what Philip Yancey's friend painfully observed: "Christians get very angry toward other Christians who sin differently than they do."[5]

11. *If you aren't broken by the cross of Jesus Christ, the Bible can be an instrument of death in your hands.* "The letter kills, but the Spirit gives life," said Paul (2 Corinthians 3:6). Wielding the Bible with unbroken flesh is a dangerous thing.

12. *If your correction of your brother or sister hurts them more than it hurts you, you probably haven't corrected in Christ.*

13. *If you do not correct someone in gentleness and utter humility, there's an excellent chance that you will fall into the same temptation or worse.* Many years ago, I remember reading a book by Watchman Nee where he said that, in his experience, anytime a believer corrected another believer with a judgmental, self-righteous attitude, the believer who did the correcting later fell into something equally serious or worse. Paul said as much (1 Corinthians 10:12; Galatians 6:1), and I've watched it myself over the years.

14. *In everything, be swift to hear the whole matter, slow to speak, slow to draw a conclusion, and slow to anger* (see James 1:19; Proverbs 18:13).[6]

   Watchman Nee aptly writes,

   > If you want your words to strike home to others, you must first be wounded yourself. Unless you have first been cut to the quick, those fine words will have no impact on your hearers. . . . How easy it is to point other people to their faults, but how hard it is to do so with tears![7]

I hope these lessons encourage you.

May we as God's servants take higher ground when we find it necessary to correct the faults of our brothers and sisters in Christ.[8]

At all costs, guard against self-righteousness. This we must do above all else.

LAW 18

Avoid Isolation

Those who handle spiritual things often suffer from spiritual loneliness and isolation. Too many pastors and teachers have no close friends. There are few people in their lives whom they can trust.

I recall speaking privately to one well-known leader. He had asked me and my friends about the kind of communities and networks we've built over the years.

When we described the type of open fellowship and mutual encouragement we have with close friends and peers, tears fell down his cheeks.

"I don't have this in my life," he confessed, "but I desperately want it."

This man's tears echoed the lament of scores of Christian leaders I've met over the years who feel painfully isolated and alone.

Isolation is not only unhealthy; it's spiritually dangerous.

All who minister need at least one or two others in their lives in whom they can confide, even if they aren't their "spiritual equals."

If you're isolated, you're constantly in your own head. And that's a frightening place to be because we cannot always trust our thoughts.

God wired us for community, even if it exists on a small scale.

Also, if you want the Lord's people to fellowship with one another as envisioned in the New Testament, you must have that same experience yourself, even if it's with just one or two others.

The Principle of Foot Washing

Allowing other believers to wash your feet is essential.

I'm not speaking of literal foot washing here. As I've shared elsewhere, foot washing in the New Testament is spiritual and holds a critical insight for remaining unpolluted from the world system.[1]

In the first century, people wore sandals, which meant their feet inevitably got dirty. The purpose of foot washing was to remove the filth from their feet.

In the same way, because we walk every day in this fallen, corrupt world, our feet will get dirty (even if we keep our noses and hands clean). It can't be prevented.

What does this look like?

You hear your coworkers gossip, run down other people, use profanity, speak obscenities, etc. Your boss gives you a hard time and doesn't value your work. You check your social media feed and racy photos pop up on your screen.

Even though you never participate in any of these behaviors, something of the fallenness of this world drags your spirit down.

What's happened?

Your feet have collected dust and dirt.

That same evening, you have coffee with a few brothers and sisters in Christ, and you begin to talk about the Lord. You even break out in a praise song.

Immediately, you feel inwardly renewed. Your spirit is refreshed, your soul restored.

What's taken place?

The dirt you collected on your feet from walking in the world has been removed. Your feet have been washed.

Having people in your life who can wash your feet and vice versa requires intentionality. Most people today don't initiate friendships. So it's on your shoulders to do so.[2]

Initiating is the easy part; finding those who will reciprocate is the challenge.

But don't lose hope. Make it a matter of prayer coupled with action.

God will supply you with a friend or two if you really desire it.

I say this out of experience.

Here's an exercise: If you feel isolated, make a list of individuals you will invite to a regular phone call or in-person coffee meeting. Pray over it and see what the Lord does.

Don't allow yourself to remain isolated.

Develop an Instinct for the Cross

Spirit-empowered ministry flows from God breaking us with the cross of Christ.

If you want to minister with God's anointing, it's vital that you develop an instinct for the cross.

I've spoken on the cross of Jesus Christ countless times, but when I speak on "bearing the cross," I have in mind something other than the Lord's atoning death for us.

I'm instead focusing on the principle of the cross—the principle of dying to oneself.

The cross has to do with denying our fallen soul life, or what some theologians call "the self-life." Your basic nature is marked by self-interest, self-preservation, and self-defense.

Jesus spoke strongly about the necessity of denying our basic nature:

> Then he said to them all: "Whoever wants to be my disciple must deny themselves and take up their cross daily and follow me. For whoever wants to save their life will lose it, but whoever loses their life for me will save it."
>
> LUKE 9:23-24

Paul also referred to the principle of dying to ourselves in both 1 Corinthians 15:31 and 2 Corinthians 4:8-12. These texts are not speaking about salvation. They are speaking about picking up a cross, carrying it daily, and following Christ in the denial of oneself.

We have all been given a cross to pick up. And God calls each of us to bear it.

Whenever your ego is touched, or your pride is exposed, or your weaknesses are pointed out—whenever you get misrepresented—the cross is ready to do its deepest work.

And you can either fight against it or die upon it.

Ten Insights About the Cross

The lessons in this chapter have come from the anvil of much personal suffering. They emerged out of many experiences of the cross in my own life.

No one should ever speak on this dimension of the cross unless they've had a steady diet of its horrendous depths. If not, what they'll share will only be bloodless theory that has little impact on people's lives.

That said, here are ten insights about bearing the cross of Christ:

1. No mere human can teach you how to recognize the cross in your life. God must show you. It's a matter of spiritual instinct.

   (Here's one clue. If you've come to the place of asking, "My God, my God, *why*?" you've undoubtedly touched the cross.)

2. The ears of God's people tend to be deaf to the cross. We don't like to hear about it.

3. The cross is the easiest thing in the world to forget. We need to be constantly reminded of it. It's like uncooked spaghetti; it just won't stick to the wall.

4. You will never know the Lord you're supposed to know outside of a rendezvous with the cross of Christ.[1]

5. Authentic body-life rarely works the way we want it to. It's a railroad track to the cross.

6. The instrument of the cross is often our fellow brethren in Christ. They unwittingly (or sometimes wittingly) hand it to us. Our family members come in a close second.

7. You cannot crucify yourself. You can drive one nail into one hand, but the other hand will remain free. Consequently, the cross is God's wonderful design.

8. God will create a tailor-made cross for you. Jesus is a carpenter, so He knows how to build them.

9. The more gifted you are, the more you need the cross in your life. You need it to break your tendency to rely on yourself, to engineer outcomes, and to exalt yourself in subtle ways.

10. In Christian community, your blind spots will eventually get exposed. True body life is a house of mirrors. The Lord will not destroy Himself within you, but He'll seek to destroy everything else. This is especially true if He has called you to His work.

Mark it down: If there is ever a time in your life to deny yourself and lose, it's when you feel someone has hurt your feelings.

The same is true when you correct someone in Christ and they not only reject it, but they retaliate by trying to defame you. When someone hates you out of jealousy, and with malice in their heart spreads vicious lies about you, you need the cross. You also need the cross when someone doesn't meet your expectations.

Christians who take offense resist the cross. And Christians who retaliate to protect their reputations and self-interests do not know the cross.

Our flesh seeks to defend itself, justify itself, get angry, lash out, and retaliate.

Sometimes it does this in passive-aggressive ways, often justifying itself with religious talk under the cloak of "God told me."

But the flesh will never sacrifice itself or absorb the blows. Instead, it will be quick to sacrifice others on the altar of one's feelings.

The flesh *always* seeks to protect one's reputation at the expense of others.

Those who do not know the cross cannot tolerate loss, suffering, or correction. And they can't remain silent. Instead, they'll allow themselves to react carnally, even calling their reaction "being led by the Spirit."

But this is deception.

These reactions are the fruit of an unbroken person who has made himself or herself top priority, refusing to take the high road, which the Spirit of the Lamb will always lead us to do.

Keep this in mind: You can waste the Lord's transformation in your life by fighting the cross.

I've watched men called of God blow it at the first press of the cross in their lives. They wrung their hands and fell to pieces after the initial flare of trouble.

The religious leaders of Jesus' day—most notably the Pharisees—were dead men walking. They could not abide the cross but embodied religious flesh on display.

The cross of Christ bids us to die, to lose, to surrender. By contrast, the flesh will do everything it can to stay alive and protect itself.

The eleven disciples ran at breakneck speed when they saw the cross emerging on a hill. They headed for the hills while the women stayed with Jesus.

Our flesh seeks to do the same whenever the cross shows up in our lives.

Crucifying the Ego

One of the hardest elements of the cross is to crucify our egos. Some men, by virtue of their upbringing, have a deep-seated insecurity. Insecurity is a highly dangerous trait, especially for someone called to the ministry.

Throughout my life, I've known two profoundly gifted speakers who were terribly insecure. This made them thrive on verbal admiration. But no number of compliments was ever enough to fill their internal black holes.

Their insecurity caused them to feel threatened by others who were also gifted. And when such people were praised by others, it fueled a mad jealousy within their hearts.

This is what deep insecurity does to a person. And this is why the ego must be put to death.

Some of the most talented people in the world are egomaniacs with inferiority complexes. Unfortunately, this is true of some of the most spiritually gifted people who ever lived.

But it gets worse.

It's possible for a person to know how to say and do the right things when confronted on a serious issue in their lives, and yet not sincerely own the issue.

In such cases, their heart betrays their words (which never get beyond the surface). And that which they count dearest to them—namely, their own work—never gets placed on the altar.

A person can look good on wood, going through the outward motions of dying on the cross, yet still be fully alive.

All told, be intentional about sharpening your instinct to lose rather than win. Not just outwardly before others, but inwardly.

The war within your own heart is the one that counts.

It is through death that we enter into life. And it is by losing that we see the Lord win.

Going to the cross is not a onetime trip for the Christian leader, either. You will have countless opportunities to die.

As I've often said, your destiny is the Lord's history. You and I will pass through all the things that Jesus passed through during His earthly life (except for the atonement).

Jesus had a wilderness, a Gethsemane, and a Judas. And so will you.

The same is true for His death and resurrection, both of which we will share if we continue to follow Him (Philippians 3:10).

The cross was not a onetime event in our Savior's life. It shows up on every page of the Gospels. Jesus constantly laid down His life, lost, and denied Himself. And He taught us to do the same.

There's a lot of talk about servant leadership today. However, leading servants have always been a rare commodity in the body of Christ.

It is only in laying hold of the Lord's indwelling life and bearing His cross that we can experience real servitude.

Only a broken man or woman serves others. But watching a brother or sister in Christ get broken is a horrible experience, and I don't enjoy seeing it.

The cross doesn't sell well. The agony and humiliation that one must go through to become a broken vessel are beyond comprehension. I've never met a woman or man of spiritual depth who hasn't been shamed and brought lower than they ever dreamed.

But this is the work of the cross.

It takes the cross of Jesus Christ to burn out religious ambition, pride, jealousy, self-seeking, and the rest of the ugly things that mark our flesh.

The cross is required for brokenness, and brokenness is required for a ministry that's marked by God's power. I cannot alter that principle, and neither can you.

Fire and Blood

The church of Jesus Christ is built on the death of a man—spiritually, emotionally, and physically. I've seen this tested by fire in the lives of many servants of God who have gone through blood up to the horse's bit.

If your work is to have any quality at all, it will come out of death.

I wrote the following email to an individual in ministry who sought my advice at a low point in his life.

> You're an incredibly bright man . . . don't ever think
> differently or short-change yourself. At the same time, those
> who possess your talents must be careful not to employ
> their cleverness to take advantage of others. Rest secure in

who God has made you. Insecurity breeds disaster in the lives of others . . . always. A man has got to know his own limitations, soberly embrace his strengths, and rest content in Christ in the midst of both. Put another way: What a man builds with his gifts, he can just as quickly destroy by his character.

Ironically, this man had filled his head with teachings on the cross. He even preached about it. As I write this book, however, he has left the Lord and is overflowing with anger and bitterness.

Never confuse spiritual gifting with spiritual life. Gifts operate despite one's character, but spiritual life requires growth in character. King Saul prophesied by the Spirit of God (gift).[2] Yet not long after, he killed the holy priests of the Lord (a cataclysmic defect in character).[3]

Ministers of God's Word who are worth their salt understand that character and spiritual life are far more important than gifts. Consequently, they have an instinct for the cross.

So take up your electric chair and your whipping post and choose to suffer and die. This is the path to God's power.

May the Lord in His mercy extract from us everything that makes us dangerous to the kingdom of God.

LAW 20

Don't Put Too Much Trust in Others

Trust must be earned and proven over time.

> Do not put your trust in princes,
>   in human beings, who cannot save.
> When their spirit departs, they return to the ground;
>   on that very day their plans come to nothing.
>
> PSALM 146:3-4

If you put your trust in people prematurely, disaster will often follow. You'll find yourself spending a great deal of time pulling knives out of your back.

Love and trust aren't the same. You can love people without trusting them.

The only perfect Person who ever lived didn't trust everyone:

> But Jesus would not entrust himself to them, for he knew all people.
>
> JOHN 2:24

Yet Jesus remained vulnerable. He chose Judas as one of His first followers, knowing both the man's character and what he would later do.

Be careful who you trust. Learn to be discerning. And never be in a rush.

If you move in haste to partner with others in ministry without establishing a basis for trust, you may live to regret it. As the old Russian proverb puts it, *doveryai, no proveryai*—trust, but verify.

In short, one way to deplete spiritual power from your life is to trust the wrong people.

Colliding and Moving On

Jake, a young minister, was excited about beginning his new role as the lead pastor of a large congregation. The previous lead pastor, Bill, had mentored Jake for almost a decade. When Bill stepped down from his leading role, he handed the baton to Jake.

Bill, however, remained on the church board.

That's when things turned ugly.

Bill called Jake often and told him how poorly he was running things. Even worse, Bill often cut Jake off at the kneecaps, maneuvering behind his back to get the results he wanted, results that ran counter to Jake's convictions and judgment.

Inevitably, Bill and Jake's relationship deteriorated. After Bill had consistently cut the ground out from under Jake's feet, Jake stepped down and began having serious doubts about God and the truthfulness of Scripture.

What had happened? Jake had put undue trust in Bill.

Had you asked Jake a year before if he overtrusted Bill, he would have replied, "Absolutely not. I respect Bill, but I put my trust in God."

But that statement turned out to be untrue.

Or consider the example of Waylen, who labored among a small group of Christians for years. The group admired Waylen and received immense spiritual help from him.

Over time, however, their respect for him began to dwindle. The group began listening to other preachers and were enthralled by their messages, some of which contradicted what Waylen taught.

Finally, the group wrote Waylen a letter and told him that they had moved on. They no longer wanted him ministering to them.

The news devastated Waylen. He concluded that God's people

are as fickle as the Florida weather (I live in Florida, and it's actually beyond fickle).

Waylen was so hurt that he lost the unction to minister again. He left the work of God.

In like manner, countless Christian leaders have started out in ministry with a twinkle in their eyes only to get smashed in the gears of some ecclesiastical committee they trusted.

When those we rely on fail to meet our expectations, our trust in God is severely tested. Then, and only then, do we find out if we are living for God or for others.

The lesson: Don't put too much trust in others, regardless of how gifted, kind, or seemingly mature they may appear to be. This includes those who love and appreciate you at the moment.

The sad truth is, many Christians are just as fickle as the Florida weather. And if you allow them to, they'll break your heart.

Employ Fasting with Prayer

A keen relationship exists between prayer and God's power.

Millions of trees have been killed and gallons of ink have been spilled by preachers and commentators telling us that prayer, especially for a Christian minister, is critical. Not a few of those books have left readers under three tons of guilt before they got twenty pages in.

So I'll spare you.

God's Power-Sharing Instrument

Prayer is God's power-sharing instrument. The Lord is not a detached, distant, aloof bystander in the world He created. At the same time, He typically doesn't intervene in the affairs of humans without being asked.

Strikingly, the Almighty invites fallen humans to cooperate with Him in bringing about His will in the earth. How marvelous and incredible!

> For we are co-workers in God's service.
> I CORINTHIANS 3:9

> Then the disciples went out and preached everywhere, and the Lord worked with them.[1]
> MARK 16:20

Prayer, then, is the mechanism by which God releases His power into the world. Through prayer, we load the missiles of the Holy Spirit to descend on the planet.

But prayer takes on a fresh dimension of power when we couple it with fasting.

By abstaining from food, we deny our flesh and strengthen our human spirit, the dwelling place of God's Spirit.

Jesus launched His ministry immediately after a long fast, where He returned to Galilee "in the power of the Spirit."

> When the devil had finished all this tempting, he left him until an opportune time. Jesus returned to Galilee in the power of the Spirit, and news about him spread through the whole countryside.
>
> LUKE 4:13-14

Overeating kills spiritual power. Fasting increases it.

I learned this by experience in my early twenties. As I prepared to attend a family wedding, I sensed the Lord wanted to use me there.

With joy, I anticipated the opportunity.

At the wedding dinner, however, I overate. I felt bloated, uncomfortable, overfull.

I suddenly realized that my spiritual energy had vanished. I felt disconnected from God, depleted of any spiritual power.

Regrettably, I lost an opportunity to minister. I'll never forget the lesson.

For that reason, whenever I'm slated to minister, I eat very little beforehand. Sometimes I don't eat at all. I save eating for afterwards.

By the same token, I sometimes fast a day, two days, or even three days before a significant time of ministry.

I'm referring to an all-water fast, the most common fast in the Bible.

On the positive side, shortly after I was converted to Christ in my teens, I fasted for several days. Remarkably, God answered five of my prayers after the fast.

It was an early lesson on the power of fasting.

Increase Our Faith

Throughout Scripture, we find Jesus releasing divine power through faith. It takes faith for people to receive God's power, and it takes faith to exercise it.

When the disciples asked Jesus why they couldn't cast out a demon, Jesus replied,

> Because of your unbelief; for assuredly, I say to you, if you have faith as a mustard seed, you will say to this mountain, "Move from here to there," and it will move; and nothing will be impossible for you. However, this kind does not go out except by prayer and fasting.
>
> MATTHEW 17:20-21, NKJV

The robust tool of fasting increases our faith. Why? Because by its very nature, fasting is an exercise in humility. We cause the flesh to die so the spirit can grow stronger.

In the book of Luke, the disciples said to the Lord, "Increase our faith!" (Luke 17:5).

Jesus didn't reply, "That's easy, gentlemen. Pray more, read your Bible more, name it and claim it, blab it and grab it," or any such thing.

Hear the Lord's surprising response:

> If you have faith as small as a mustard seed, you can say to this mulberry tree, "Be uprooted and planted in the sea," and it will obey you.
>
> Suppose one of you has a servant plowing or looking after the sheep. Will he say to the servant when he comes in from the field, "Come along now and sit down to eat"? Won't he

rather say, "Prepare my supper, get yourself ready and wait on me while I eat and drink; after that you may eat and drink"? Will he thank the servant because he did what he was told to do? So you also, when you have done everything you were told to do, should say, "We are unworthy servants; we have only done our duty."

LUKE 17:6-10

In this passage, Jesus appears to be saying that the way to increase our faith is to humble ourselves.[2]

We are all unworthy to serve the King of the universe. So there's nothing by which we can boast. Service is merely our calling.

In today's celebrity culture, many Christian leaders reverse the principle of this parable. They feel entitled *because* they are servants of God. So they delight in being served rather than viewing themselves as unworthy servants.

But the path to God's power is through faith, and the way to increase our faith is by humbling ourselves under God's mighty hand, recognizing ourselves to be unprofitable servants.

Fasting is one of the chief doorways into this humble state, which is why it increases God's power.

In short, a powerful connection exists between spiritual power and faith. Fasting increases one's faith, while overeating depletes it.

Note, too, that the results of a fast often come after the fast ends, rather than during it (in my experience, at least).

One last observation: On a fast, our carnal urges diminish drastically. This includes quieting the libido. Consequently, fasting—coupled with a few other ingredients—is highly effective in breaking addictions.[3]

The best book I know of on the subject of fasting is Arthur Wallis's *God's Chosen Fast*. I recommend that every person in ministry read it at least once.[4]

Discern the Season

Word versus Spirit debates, along with outreach versus community-building scuffles, are both unfruitful and unnecessary.

Each debate builds its premise by asking the wrong question.

"What's more important, God's written Word (Scripture) or the Holy Spirit?" they ask, or, "What should we focus on more, evangelism or building the believing community?"

In both cases, those are the wrong questions.

The right question is, "What season are we in right now?"

God put seasons in His creation as object lessons to illustrate the spiritual life, both for the individual as well as for a local body of believers.

Consequently, over the years, I've learned to discern the season.

There is a season for outreach and a season for in-reach (building the community).

There is a season for sowing and a season for reaping.

There are seasons of labor and seasons of rest.

There is a season to begin a new work and a season to stop a work.

The question before the house is always, "What season am I in? What season is my ministry in? What season is my local fellowship in right now?"

I learned this lesson on two fronts.

First, I've watched many churches never get beyond shallow relationships and superficial spiritual growth, all because they were taught that they had to constantly evangelize.

The people in these churches, aside from having no depth in their connections with others in the fellowship, ended up burning out.

On the flip side, churches that focused exclusively on community-building turned into insular backwaters with no impact on their cities or towns. They eventually died due to a lack of "new blood."

Second, I've watched many pastors, Bible teachers, and seminary professors lose their excitement and passion for God and His work. They came to a place where they just recycled the same old material.

Speaking became drudgery—robotic, mechanical, lifeless.

They didn't realize that the season had changed and the time had come for them to adjust.

In my own ministry, whenever I feel the energy, excitement, and life starting to wane in relation to a project or routine, I know it's time to shift gears and pick up something else.

The season has changed, and I must move with it if I'm going to bear fruit.

A Man for All Seasons

Discerning the season also means being a man or woman for *all* seasons.

> Preach the word; be prepared in season and out of season;
> correct, rebuke and encourage—with great patience and
> careful instruction.
>
> 2 TIMOTHY 4:2

The King James Version puts it this way: "be instant in season, out of season."

To be instant in season and out of season means that you are always ready to serve as the Spirit of God leads, regardless of the season you're in.

You could be in a personal dry spell, where the sand is blowing in your face, your feet are burning, and your lips are parched from the scorching sun. The Bible reads like the *Wall Street Journal*, the earth is hard, the heavens are brass, and it seems like God is on vacation.

To be instant in season and out means that even in dry spells and during crises when you're walking through the ninth circle of hell, you're still ready to minister Christ.

True ministry, then, isn't a "show," where you're "on" some days and "off" others. Neither is it an occupation in which you're allotted "work" days and "vacation" days.

No, ministry is a vocation that encompasses your entire life.

As a minister of God's Word, you are always "on," always ready to follow the Spirit and serve.

As we end this chapter, I encourage you to take the temperature and ask yourself: "What spiritual season am I in right now? What am I to focus on presently in my ministry and in my personal life?"

By the way, if you're looking for a footnote, just ask Solomon:

There is a time for everything,
    and a season for every activity under the heavens:

    a time to be born and a time to die,
    a time to plant and a time to uproot,
    a time to kill and a time to heal,
    a time to tear down and a time to build,
    a time to weep and a time to laugh,
    a time to mourn and a time to dance,
    a time to scatter stones and a time to gather them,
    a time to embrace and a time to refrain from embracing,
    a time to search and a time to give up,
    a time to keep and a time to throw away,
    a time to tear and a time to mend,
    a time to be silent and a time to speak,
    a time to love and a time to hate,
    a time for war and a time for peace.

ECCLESIASTES 3:1-8

When the seasons change in both spiritual life and ministry, you either roll with it or you get crushed under it.

Resist Bitterness

One of the surest ways to destroy your spiritual life, as well as your ministry, is to become bitter.

If you allow bitterness to take root in your heart, there is no treatment for it.

> See to it that no one falls short of the grace of God and that no bitter root grows up to cause trouble and defile many.
> HEBREWS 12:15

Not only will bitterness sink your ship; it will drown others as well.

Attitudes are contagious, and misery loves company. If you drink the poison of bitterness, you'll slowly die. But you'll also kill others because bitter people spout acid all over the earth.

Nothing so injures the human spirit as the injuries inflicted by other believers. Those wounds are the most difficult to heal. They steal the life from our spirits.

However, if you recognize this and allow the Lord to extend grace to you, you'll be set free.

Suffering Sheep Bite

"Where two or three are gathered together in My name, there will be trouble." (Isn't that in the Gospels somewhere?)

All jesting aside, sheep bite is difficult to heal. The chafing from God's people is most acute, leaving our souls raw and bleeding.

When God uses you, expect to attract religious trolls, antagonists, and flamethrowers.

Until you've gotten blasted by shrapnel from some of the "Christians" you've served, you may not understand what I'm about to say.

Very often, when we get hurt by those we've poured our lives out for, everything inside goes dark.

The Bible could have just as well been printed on blank pages.

Nothing moves inside us. There is zero spiritual registration.

At such times, there is often one thing that can help—music.

You may find something else, but you must find *something* to fill your soul when you feel your inward parts have died.

And whatever you find, stay with it.

Know this: There is still a living God, and there are still decent Christians.

Here's how I put it in *God's Favorite Place on Earth*,

> If you are a Christian, then, expect to follow in the footsteps of your Lord. You will know the scalding pain and heartbreaking disillusionment of rejection.
>
> How you respond, however, will determine if you become broken or bitter.
>
> If you view such things from a natural plane, you may get so depressed that your eyes cross, feeling that you have to climb up just to reach the bottom. These are the typical emotions that provoke grudges.
>
> Someone once said that you don't hold a grudge. It holds you. Holding a grudge is self-inflicted pain. Consequently, bitterness doesn't imprison those who hurt you. It imprisons you.
>
> Again, we do not have the strength to forgive others who wound us. But we have One who indwells us whose name is

Forgiveness. And He is able and willing to forgive through us, releasing us and others.[1]

When you're doing ministry valuable to the kingdom of God, the question is not, "Will other people ever hurt me?" The question is, "When will they hurt me?" (Sorry to rain on your parade.)

The good news is that when this happens, there's a remedy.

Pain vs. Bitterness

Pain is inevitable. It will happen. Usually at the hands of other Christians.

Bitterness, however, is a choice.

It's the difference between being punctured with a needle and picking the scab so it never heals.

Those who choose to allow bitterness to gain ground in their hearts have something else going on inside them. Something quite serious.

Typically, people become embittered when they have unrealistic expectations or selfish ulterior motives.

When their expectations aren't met or their self-seeking motives go unexposed, bitterness easily sets in.

Bitterness is also contagious.

If you're struggling with bitterness or feel on the verge of becoming embittered, the worst thing you can do is sit around with others who have grown bitter.

Such groups are often pitched as "healing" stations, but they keep the wounds open by constantly picking at them.

The fact is nothing in this universe can *make* you bitter. None of us have suffered the kind of injustice Jesus Christ did, nor the degree of physical pain He weathered at the hands of others.

So if anyone has a right to be bitter, it's Him. Yet He wasn't, and He never will be.

Here's the antidote: You must be willing to see the hand of a loving, caring God in your painful situation. This is how Joseph kept from becoming embittered toward his brothers (Genesis 50:19-20).

It's also how Jesus kept from becoming embittered toward those who lobbied for His crucifixion (Hebrews 12:2).

The willingness to accept pain and suffering under the providential hand of God is the key to resisting bitterness.

(By the way, if you believe that God isn't sovereign, this logically means that He's helpless and your trial took Him by surprise. Therefore, you're on your own. The world is haphazard, random, and you're forced to live like a practical atheist. For a theological discussion on God's relationship to our suffering, see Appendix I "Who Brought Your Trial?" in *Hang On, Let Go*.)

Shifting the Terrain

Much of what we feel and how we behave is rooted in how we think. So it really comes down to our mindset.

If you regularly think about a painful situation that caused you heartache, the remedy is to stand on a different hill and change your perspective.

One safeguard against becoming bitter and acerbic is to exercise empathy and refuse to take anything personally.[2]

When people mistreat others, they merely expose something dark within themselves. They are holding up a huge sign that says, "I have major unresolved issues."

Though you might have contributed to their feelings, how they react is on them, not you.

This insight is a game changer.

The mindset you must adopt sounds something like this:

Lee must be dealing with some internal issues. Perhaps he hates himself. Perhaps he's harboring a grudge. Perhaps he experienced deep pain and abuse during his childhood or young adulthood. He's acting out of his own insecurity, pain, and self-loathing. This isn't about me. It's about him and his issues. I've given him and his conduct to the Lord. I've surrendered the hurt I feel to my God.

There's also something else. We can't control what others do to us, but only our reaction to it. And our reaction is everything.

It will determine if mistreatment devastates or develops us.

All Christians, including spiritual leaders, who are devastated by mistreatment share the same common symptoms:

- Anger toward those who hurt them.
- The propensity to talk about it constantly, even in group settings (which spreads the bitterness like the flu).
- The unwillingness to trust anyone ever again (especially fellow leaders).
- Blaming God for allowing it to happen.

On the flip side, those who effectively resist bitterness:

- Acknowledge their pain but release it and the associated anger to the Lord.
- Shut their mouths about it, speaking to only one or two trusted people in confidence and leaving it there. They give it to God and move on.
- Recognize that while all Christians are fallible, not all are toxic. And not all leaders are unscrupulous. So they are able to trust again.
- Understand that whenever humans mean something for evil, God intends it for good. But God must be put into the equation.

> As for you, you meant evil against me, but God meant it for good.
>
> GENESIS 50:20, ESV

> And now, do not be distressed and do not be angry with yourselves for selling me here, because it was to save lives that God sent me ahead of you.
>
> GENESIS 45:5

> And we know that for those who love God all things
> work together for good, for those who are called
> according to his purpose.
> ROMANS 8:28, ESV

What follows is a practical assignment I've given elsewhere. I encourage you to try it. Remember, bitterness is like drinking poison and waiting for the other person to get sick. It hurts you, not them. If you have trouble forgiving others, try this to help you release and forgive them.

- On a sheet of paper, write the name of every person who has hurt you. Leave five spaces below each name.

- Underneath each name, write what they did to you.

- When you are finished, raise the paper up to the Lord and tell Him out loud that you are releasing these people into His hands, forgiving what they did to you.

- Burn the piece of paper and thank the Lord for His release while you watch it turn to ash.

- If what they did to you comes back into your mind, tell the Lord that those people are His and you have released them.[3]

- When it comes to overcoming bitterness, there is a vaccine. So take the jab.

LAW 24

Serve in the Spirit

There are two ways to serve God. One is to serve in the energy of the flesh; the other is to serve in the power of the Spirit.

Serving God in the flesh simply means relying on your own natural abilities, the things you received at birth—your natural talent, intelligence, gifting, charisma, etc.

Serving in the Spirit is quite different. Consider Paul's words:

> God, whom I serve in my spirit in preaching the gospel of his Son . . .
>
> ROMANS 1:9

> But now we have been released from the Law, having died to that by which we were bound, so that we serve in newness of the Spirit and not in oldness of the letter.
>
> ROMANS 7:6, NASB

Many of my books stress that the secret to our Lord's remarkable life and ministry is that He didn't live by His own natural powers. Rather, He lived by His Father's life, which indwelt Him by the Holy Spirit.

> Jesus gave them this answer: "Very truly I tell you, the Son can do nothing by himself; he can do only what he sees his Father doing, because whatever the Father does the Son also does."
>
> JOHN 5:19

> As the living Father hath sent me, and I live by the Father: so
> he that eateth me, even he shall live by me.
>
> JOHN 6:57, KJV

When it comes to God's work, the Lord forbids reliance on our natural ingenuity, skill, energy, and talent. Instead, He calls us to serve "in the Spirit," which means to completely rely on His indwelling life as the energizing force of our ministry.

It's a question of sources. But the difference is night and day. Especially in the impact your ministry will have here and in eternity. (That's not a bad title for a book, by the way!)[1]

A quote attributed to both William Booth and Hudson Taylor says, "There are three stages of every great work of God. First it's impossible, then it's difficult, then it's done."

That's an excellent description of what it means to serve God in the Spirit. It's humanly impossible. But when you look back and it's accomplished, you're not quite sure how it happened. It was Christ living through you, rather than you living by your own natural strength and energy:

> I have been crucified with Christ; it is no longer I who live,
> but Christ lives in me; and the life which I now live in the
> flesh I live by faith in the Son of God, who loved me and
> gave Himself for me.
>
> GALATIANS 2:20, NKJV

Handling Problems with Christ

You will face insurmountable problems throughout your ministry. Some of them will echo the problems Jesus and the early apostles faced. But a monumental difference exists between handling a problem with Christ and handling it with your own understanding, wisdom, cleverness, and energy.

The servant of God who handles problems with Christ draws on a power and wisdom that exceed his own.

Have you ever considered how Jesus handled hot-boiling criticism? Have you ever noticed how He got out of impossible situations?

Jesus faced those dispiriting dilemmas by relying on His Father's life, which explains why He gave such out-of-the-box responses, transcending human reason and logic.

Put another way, He lived by the tree of life rather than by the tree of the knowledge of good and evil.

T. Austin-Sparks explained it this way:

"When I took you, I not only took you as the sinner that you might regard yourself to be, but I took you as being all that you are by nature—your good as well as your bad; your abilities as well as your disabilities; yes, every resource of yours. I took you as a worker, a preacher, an organizer! My Cross means that not even for Me can you be or do anything out from yourself, but if there is to be anything at all it must be out from Me, and that means a life of absolute dependence and faith."

At this point, therefore, we awoke to the fundamental principle of our Lord's own life while here, and it became the law of everything for us from that time. That principle was: "nothing of (out from) Himself," but "all things of (out from) God."

"The Son can do nothing of (out from) Himself, but what He seeth the Father doing: for what things soever He doeth, then the Son also doeth in like manner" (John 5:19).

"I can of Myself do nothing: as I hear I judge" (John 5:30).

"My teaching is not Mine, but His that sent Me" (John 7:16).[2]

Though this principle is foreign language to many ministers today, it's clear as day in 2 Corinthians 4, which I regard as the basic "textbook" for Ministry 101.

The work of Christ's cross, when applied to your natural life, is designed to break your dependence on what you are by nature.

Consider the words of Peter:

> As each one has received a gift, minister it to one another, as good stewards of the manifold grace of God. If anyone speaks, let him speak as the oracles of God. If anyone ministers, let him do it as with the ability which God supplies, that in all things God may be glorified through Jesus Christ, to whom belong the glory and the dominion forever and ever. Amen.
>
> I PETER 4:10-11, NKJV

Notice that Peter says to minister with the ability that God provides. The New Living Translation puts it this way: "Do it with all the strength and energy that God supplies."

This statement is a clear reference to relying on Christ's life and power rather than our own.

A naturally gifted person will feel tempted to lean on his gifts when he ministers. But whenever he does this, people will be impressed with his gifting, not with the Lord or His power.

Read carefully these words by Paul:

> For I resolved to know nothing while I was with you except Jesus Christ and him crucified. I came to you in weakness with great fear and trembling. My message and my preaching were not with wise and persuasive words, but with a demonstration of the Spirit's power, so that your faith might not rest on human wisdom, but on God's power.
>
> I CORINTHIANS 2:2-5

Paul resisted the impulse to draw on his natural speaking gifts because he knew that if he did, those who heard him would place their confidence in human wisdom and strength.

Instead, Paul understood that the secret to releasing God's power was to be desperate, refusing to trust his own giftedness, but instead, relying fully on the power of God.

Serving in the Spirit rather than in the energy of the flesh is one of the key ingredients to having spiritual power.

A large part of that is to be suspect of your own giftedness and desperately depend on God's power "with great fear and trembling."

LAW 25

Defy the Conventional Wisdom

The church of Jesus Christ is dying from a lack of imagination and creativity.

The average minister today has grown up in a system that never dares to do things differently.

I'm talking about its practices, not its doctrines.

Countless pastors cannot seem to think beyond the five-hundred-year-old Protestant worship service given to us by John Calvin. And yet it's losing people by the droves.[1]

The Lord is looking for servants willing to defy the conventional wisdom in every arena—whether ministry, evangelism, church, fellowship, prayer, discipleship, Bible reading, leadership, books, blogs, podcasts, advertising, or whatever.

The most spiritually powerful people I've ever known defied the conventional wisdom, knowing full well the consequences.

They resisted the status quo. They persisted in ripping up the soil and turning the sod. They were unafraid to overturn the apple cart.

The Christian camp today often lags far behind the world in regard to exceptional art and creativity. This ought not to be, since the Founder of our faith is the most creative Person in existence.[2]

To better explain what I mean by defying the conventional wisdom, I'll take the liberty of using an example from the secular world.

Many music critics have ranked Led Zeppelin as the greatest rock band in history. The band didn't follow Christ, so I don't endorse their lifestyle, their beliefs, or the energy they relied upon. (So there's no need to send me nasty emails!)

DEFY THE CONVENTIONAL WISDOM ‖ 119

But they were creative geniuses. And we can glean three lessons from them in this regard:

1. ***Don't sell out to pop culture.*** Zeppelin didn't compromise their values for the sake of pop culture. Consequently, the band refused to cut singles (at least in the UK). They felt that if someone wanted to get into their work, they had to buy their albums.

   An album, like a book, represents a full body of work. "Take the whole thing or leave it," was their position.

   In this regard, Zep went against the grain of all other bands during their era. The musicians stayed true to their art. They wanted to be an underground band, thus they seldom did interviews. *Rolling Stone* (the voice of the music establishment at the time) treated them brutally.

   Takeaway: If you want your messages, books, blog, music, or any other kind of art to be hugely popular, then make it "pop."

   But if you want to stay true to your message, convictions, and vision, go for depth. Refuse to appease the establishment, and leave the results with God.

   Ironically, Led Zeppelin had a profound, even seminal, influence on contemporary music. Zep's music changed the face of the rock world, even though they refused to go "pop."

   While staying true to your art might grab the multitudes, it usually doesn't. Your calling is to stay true to yourself and faithful to your calling. That's your goal (1 Corinthians 4:2; Luke 16:10-12).

2. ***Don't be afraid to debunk the conventional wisdom.*** For their fourth album, Zep decided to do something that had never been done before or since. They gave their album no title. And they didn't even put the band's name on it!

   Their record company said this was "commercial suicide."

Yet Led Zeppelin IV (which is what fans called it) went on to sell over thirty-two million copies and has been hailed as one of the greatest albums in music history.

Takeaway: Don't be afraid to run against the conventional wisdom. Dare to do the unthinkable and that which has never been done before. Not for shock value but because it's in your heart to do so. Follow your convictions, not the praises of mortals.

3. *Speak well of your competitors.* In 1970, Zep surpassed the Beatles in popularity. When the press asked the band members about this, they had only good things to say about "The Fab Four."

At the end of one interview, Jimmy Page, the lead guitarist and founder of Led Zeppelin, was asked, "How do you feel about the Beatles?"

"I think they're great," he replied. "They've made some fantastic statements." Such well-speaking about one's peers and competitors is profoundly admirable. Unfortunately, we seldom see this among Christian ministers today.

More often we see the opposite, more like Elvis's alleged posture toward the Beatles.

According to Ringo Starr, though Elvis treated the Beatles nicely in person, the "king" of rock and roll tried to have them deported when their monumental success threatened him.

What makes this even more disturbing is that the Beatles idolized Elvis and regarded him as a distant mentor. Tragically, in the Christian world, it's not uncommon for mentors to turn on their mentees when they excel them. (Think Saul and David.)

Takeaway: Always speak well of your competitors and even your enemies. (I read the New Testament once, and Jesus had something to say about this in Matthew 5:44 and Paul in Romans 12:14, 19-21. "Bless" means to "speak well of.")

You can always find something complimentary to say about another believer without damning them with faint praise.

I've taken flak from some Christians when I've publicly spoken well about someone who was throwing spears at me. People expected me to mount a counterattack instead of responding positively.

They had no idea what I was doing or why. But taking the high ground should never become a lost art in the Christian world.

Benjamin Franklin put it beautifully: "I resolve to speak ill of no man whatever, not even in a matter of truth; but rather by some means excuse the faults I hear charged upon others, and upon proper occasions speak all the good I know of everybody."[3]

When it comes to creativity, there are only two options. Be a cog in the wheel or learn from those who have blazed fresh trails ahead of you.

You decide.

Keep Your Hands Clean

Separation from the world is a first principle in the spiritual life. Though Jesus touched lepers, His hands remained clean.

He was called the "friend of sinners," yet Hebrews says He was "set apart from sinners" (Matthew 11:19; Hebrews 7:26).

Our Lord befriended the worst transgressors, but He always kept His hands pure.

> Who may ascend the mountain of the LORD?
>> Who may stand in his holy place?
> The one who has clean hands and a pure heart.
>
> PSALM 24:3-4

> Whoever walks in integrity walks securely,
>> but whoever takes crooked paths will be found out.
>
> PROVERBS 10:9

> The integrity of the upright guides them,
>> but the unfaithful are destroyed by their duplicity.
>
> PROVERBS 11:3

In a similar way, the servant of the Lord must remain separate from the world (see 2 Corinthians 6:14–7:1).

At the same time, he or she must be willing to engage those enslaved by the world.

All servants of God must learn to touch unclean people while keeping their hands clean. Consider Paul's sober exhortation to Timothy:

> Now in a great house there are not only vessels of gold and silver but also of wood and clay, some for honorable use, some for dishonorable. Therefore, if anyone cleanses himself from what is dishonorable, he will be a vessel for honorable use, set apart as holy, useful to the master of the house, ready for every good work.
>
> 2 TIMOTHY 2:20-21, ESV

Remember, it's not just the blatant sins that dirty our hands; it's the little foxes that spoil the vine (Song of Solomon 2:15).

Keeping one's hands clean dips into other areas besides sin and worldliness. It also involves the area of handling money.

Sordid Gain

The New Testament speaks loudly about something called "sordid gain." And its warnings against it are particularly pointed at those who teach:

> There are many . . . empty talkers and deceivers . . . who must be silenced because they are upsetting whole families, teaching things they should not teach for the sake of sordid gain.
>
> TITUS 1:10-11, NASB (1995)

> Shepherd the flock of God among you, exercising oversight not under compulsion, but voluntarily, according to the will of God; and not for sordid gain, but with eagerness.
>
> 1 PETER 5:2, NASB (1995)

> For the overseer must be above reproach as God's steward,
> not self-willed, not quick-tempered, not addicted to wine,
> not pugnacious, not fond of sordid gain.
>
> TITUS 1:7, NASB (1995)

Sordid gain refers to "dishonest" gain, or what the King James Version calls "filthy lucre."

When Paul said he hadn't "coveted anyone's silver or gold or clothing," he ran against the grain of those who fleeced the flock (Acts 20:33).

Paul didn't seek the possessions of those to whom he ministered (2 Corinthians 12:14).

So how should God's servants handle money?

Who you receive offerings and donations from is part of the mix.

Wealthy donors, for instance, rarely give freely. Their gifts usually come with strings attached, strings of expectation and control.

How about taking donations from unbelievers?

> It was for the sake of the Name that they went out, receiving
> no help from the pagans.
>
> 3 JOHN 1:7

In this text, John has in mind the itinerant workers who traveled to preach the gospel for the sake of Jesus ("the Name"). These workers refused to receive financial help from the people to whom they preached the gospel—pagans (unbelievers).

Believe it or not, when unbelievers give to God's work, they often feel that God accepts them regardless of how they live. Financial donations give such people a false sense of spiritual assurance.

Questions to Consider

Frank Laubach, a man who consistently operated in God's power, made this insightful remark:

Even when we invite him [Jesus] into the main room of our
heart, we often keep him out of some hidden little room in
the mind's cellar, where we try to hide sly secrets from him
and from the world. . . . This is why we do not feel the sense
of his approval and why we lack power.[1]

Consider several soul-searching questions that touch on areas in
which many ministers lose their way.

I encourage you to squarely face each question.

- What are those hidden little rooms in your mind and heart
  that you've shut the Lord out of?
- Will you dirty your hands by accepting donations from those
  who attach strings (spoken or unspoken) to their giving?
- Will you take money from those to whom you should give the
  gospel freely (Matthew 10:8)?
- Will you refuse to misuse any money given to you, your
  fellowship, and your ministry?
- Will you resist making decisions based on financial security
  and preserving your ministerial identity?

Upton Sinclair rightly said, "It is difficult to get a man to understand
something, when his salary depends upon his not understanding it!"[2]

Many ministers find the lure of money a temptation too strong
to resist. The servant whom God uses mightily, however, keeps his or
her hands clean, including in the area of money.

Such individuals aren't perfect by any means. Nor are they free
from mistakes. But they don't base their decisions on money, security,
pleasure, name, fame, or game.

They are in it for the Lord's glory and nothing else.

This principle even moves into small areas like tipping (a custom
practiced in the USA).

Do you tip your waitress or waiter the bare minimum, or do you tip generously, recognizing that such small actions speak volumes about what you truly believe about God?

The epistles overflow with exhortations about not bringing a reproach on the Lord's name by how we act in front of the world. Paul often exhorted God's people to conduct themselves in a godly manner toward unbelievers "so that God's name and our teaching may not be slandered" (1 Timothy 6:1).

Consider the following:

> Keep your conduct among the Gentiles honorable, so that when they speak against you as evildoers, they may see your good deeds and glorify God on the day of visitation.
> I PETER 2:12, ESV

> An overseer must be above reproach. . . . Moreover, he must be well thought of by outsiders, so that he may not fall into disgrace, into a snare of the devil.
> I TIMOTHY 3:2, 7, ESV

T. Austin-Sparks sums up this law:

> The Lord calls for distinctiveness of life and testimony, real distinctiveness of life and testimony. Is our life, dear friends, is your life and my life in this world in our connections and associations and so on, quite distinct, no mistaking to what realm we belong, to Whom we belong?[3]

If you've blown it in this area, don't fret. You're not alone. Simply repent, receive the Lord's forgiveness, and walk forward.

With God as our Help, let's keep our hands clean.

LAW 27

Unveil Christ

I've often said that good preachers leave people saying, "What a good message," while great preachers leave them saying, "Wow! What a Christ!"

Your job as a minister of the gospel is to unveil the Lord Jesus Christ. It's to point all your arrows toward Him, introducing Him to both the saved and the unsaved in fresh ways that steal their hearts and send their souls into adoring surrender.

Your task is to preach a *Him*, not an *it*. In *From Eternity to Here*, I put it like this:

> In the first eight years of my Christian experience, I learned to major in a slew of "Christian" things. And that is my point—they were things.
>
> All of the churches and movements I was involved in had effectively preached to me an *it*. Evangelism is an *it*. The power of God is an *it*. Eschatology is an *it*. Christian theology is an *it*. Christian doctrine is an *it*. Faith is an *it*. Apologetics is an *it*.
>
> I made the striking discovery that I don't need an *it*. I have never needed an *it*. And I will never need an *it*. Christian *its*, no matter how good or true, eventually wear out, run dry, and become tiresome.
>
> I don't need an *it*, I need a *Him*!
> And so do you.
> We do not need things. We need Jesus Christ.[1]

For this reason, Paul constantly refers to Christ throughout all his letters. For example:

- Colossians 1 (twenty-nine verses): thirty references to Christ
- Ephesians 1 (twenty-three verses): twenty-six references
- Philippians 1 (thirty verses): twenty references
- Romans 1:1-9: eleven references
- 1 Corinthians 1:1-10: thirteen references
- 2 Corinthians 1:1-5: five references
- Galatians 1:1-4: four references

Paul was obsessed with his Lord. He was also a man full of the Spirit, and the Spirit is occupied with Christ.

And yet, when I hear preachers and teachers today, so many mention Christ only once or twice in a typical message. Worse still, many never mention Him at all.

At best, He gets honorable mention and nothing more.

These individuals preach and teach an *it*, not a *Him*.

Both believers and unbelievers need a sublime revealing of Jesus that astonishes the heart and sets it into awe.

Your mission, therefore, is to flood people with Christ so that those who hear you get washed away in the glory of God.

Preach Him until they are left staggering, until they are intoxicated with their Lord. Preach Christ until He runs out of their ears. Exalt Him beyond exaltation. Drown them in the knowledge and revelation of the Lord Jesus. Reveal Him so they get an internal sighting of His glory. Then show them how to know Him.

It is Christ and Christ alone who captures the heart. For this reason, when you unveil Him, you don't have to tell God's people to be more devoted or committed. If you reveal Jesus like they've never seen or heard before and they catch a fresh glimpse of Him, they will be committed and devoted.

When God's people get saturated with Christ in message and experience, they also have a good shot at freedom. The book of Galatians argues that when we start following rules, we are in our flesh. Without a revelation of Christ, we will always revert to legalism or libertinism.[2]

Unfortunately, men and women who can preach Christ like I've described are in short supply today.

The Unsearchable Riches

A large part of my ministry involves removing obstacles.

I've told this story elsewhere, but an admirer once asked Michelangelo how he sculpted the famous statue of David that now sits in Florence, Italy.

"I first fixed my attention on the slab of raw marble," Michelangelo replied. "I studied it, and then I chipped away all that wasn't David."

Michelangelo's answer aptly describes New Testament ministry. We declare Christ on the one hand and remove everything that's not Christ on the other.

> But when God, who set me apart from my mother's
> womb and called me by his grace, was pleased to reveal
> his Son in me so that I might preach him among the
> Gentiles, my immediate response was not to consult any
> human being.
> GALATIANS 1:15-16

Peter had a very similar experience. After he publicly confessed Jesus as the Messiah, the Son of the living God, Jesus replied with these words:

> Blessed are you, Simon Bar-Jonah! For flesh and blood has
> not revealed this to you, but my Father who is in heaven.
> MATTHEW 16:17, ESV

Notice the word *revealed*.

This revelation, or inward seeing of Jesus, is what enabled Paul to preach what he called "the unsearchable riches of Christ" and to "bring to light for everyone" the mystery of the ages, which is God's eternal purpose.

> To me, though I am the very least of all the saints, this grace was given, to preach to the Gentiles the unsearchable riches of Christ, and to bring to light for everyone what is the plan of the mystery hidden for ages in God, who created all things.
> EPHESIANS 3:8-9, ESV

A central part of God's eternal purpose is the titanic, explosive, life-altering gospel of the kingdom—a message that shakes the universe to its foundations.[3]

Let me ask: Is your ministry marked by preaching the unsearchable riches of Christ? Do you bring to light the mystery of God's eternal purpose? Do you unfold the gospel of the kingdom? Are people awestruck after you minister Christ to them?

If you answer "no," then may I challenge you to ask whether you're preaching the apostolic message of the New Testament?

The good news is that we can solve this problem.

If we are to preach the unfathomable riches of Christ in a living way, we must first receive such an unveiling of Jesus in our own hearts.

We need a revelation of Christ that burns in our being and motivates us to do nothing but preach Him until God's people are floored. Listen to Paul's prayer:

> I keep asking that the God of our Lord Jesus Christ, the glorious Father, may give you the Spirit of wisdom and revelation, so that you may know him better.
> EPHESIANS 1:17

Both sinners and saints need Christ beyond everything else. Christ alone transforms. We must therefore declare Him in all we preach and teach.

If you grasp this, you'll be in a position to bring jaw-dropping, spellbinding messages that reveal the glories of Jesus in a way that astounds those who hear.

If you have a heart hungry to receive a revelation of Christ, a moment will come when you see Him—and you'll never recover. And that "sighting" will drive you for the rest of your life.

You'll also possess a new gauge by which to evaluate if Christ is being proclaimed or not. You'll hear someone preach, and your spirit will say, "That's not Christ," or, "That's my Lord!"

On this score, A. B. Simpson rightly said, "Preaching without spiritual aroma is like a rose without fragrance. We can only get the perfume by getting more of Christ."[4]

"This all sounds great, Frank, but how do I receive an unveiling of Christ to my heart so that I can preach Him with power and reality?"

Receiving an unveiling of Christ isn't a matter of *add water, stir, and microwave on high for two minutes*. The best I can do is give you a beginning.

First, seek the Father for an unveiling of Jesus Christ to your heart. Seek and keep seeking. Knock and keep knocking. Ask and keep asking. Don't let up until, at last, you apprehend Him like never before.

Second, actively look for Christ when you read Scripture. Consider these texts:

> You search the Scriptures because you think they give you eternal life. But the Scriptures point to me!
>
> JOHN 5:39, NLT

> All Scripture is God-breathed and is useful for teaching, rebuking, correcting and training in righteousness, so that the servant of God may be thoroughly equipped for every good work.
>
> 2 TIMOTHY 3:16-17

I am the light of the world. . . .

The entrance of Your words gives light;
It gives understanding to the simple.
JOHN 8:12; PSALM 119:130, NKJV

The servant of God is "equipped for every good work" only when he or she finds Christ in the text. All God-breathed Scripture points to Jesus. Cut the Bible in any place, and it will bleed Christ.[5]

Third, ask the Spirit of God to fill you. Not just once or twice, but every time you plan to stand up (or sit down) to preach or teach.

Paul exhorted the churches in Asia minor,

And do not get drunk with wine, for that is debauchery, but be filled with the Spirit.
EPHESIANS 5:18, ESV

Sixty percent of our physical bodies are made up of water. However, we still need to drink water daily to survive. For this reason, some specialists encourage us to drink sixty ounces of water per day.

All throughout Scripture, water is a picture of the Spirit of Christ (John 7:37-39; 4:14; Revelation 21:6; 1 Corinthians 10:4; 12:13; Exodus 17:6).

After you entrusted your life to Jesus, Christ came to indwell you by His Spirit. But just like natural water, if you don't keep drinking from the Spirit, you will become spiritually dehydrated.

Consequently, drink of God's Spirit every day, and let Him fill you with His power.

The Holy Spirit is God's personal presence. The main function of the Holy Spirit is to reveal, magnify, and glorify Jesus Christ (John 15:26; 16:14-15). All of His guidance in our lives is toward that end.

A Spirit-filled minister, then, will unveil Christ.

Incidentally, the key requirements to being filled with the power of the Spirit are confession, renunciation, surrender, obedience, and faith.[6]

Fourth, expose yourself to those who unveil Christ when they minister. Listen to them over and over again.[7]

Alas, there are innumerable preachers and teachers on the earth today, but very few preach Christ out of a personal unveiling. So I encourage you to make this your goal. Let Jesus obsess and possess you.

Paul stated his aim in ministry like this:

> He [Christ] is the one we proclaim, admonishing and
> teaching everyone with all wisdom, so that we may present
> everyone fully mature in Christ.
> COLOSSIANS 1:28

There's more, but these four steps will give you a solid beginning. A quote often attributed to Antoine de Saint-Exupéry sums up your task as a preacher of Jesus Christ:

> If you want to build a ship, don't drum up the men to gather
> wood, divide the work, and give orders. Instead, teach them
> to yearn for the vast and endless sea.[8]

Jesus Christ is an endless sea. Discover how to know Him more deeply and declare Him richly so your hearers will yearn for Him— now and forevermore, world without end.[9]

LAW 28

Manage Conflict

I shudder when I meet young men just starting out in ministry who think that what awaits them is glory, prestige, honor, and blessing.

Let me turn that idea on its head using some stark terms for which I won't apologize.

The work of God is a death sentence. It's designed to destroy you.[1]

By that, I mean it's intended to break your ego, crucify your flesh, and kill your "need" to impress or control others (a common trait among many men and women in ministry today).

While the Lord's work has many joys, it's more like a winepress than a picnic. Put another way, it's an occupational hazard.

If you are making a dent in the kingdom of darkness, you will find yourself on the raw, bleeding edge of conflict. You will face lit torches accompanied by pitchforks. And most of it will not come from the lost. It will come from the religious world.

This shouldn't surprise you. Jesus, Paul, and every other person who raised a standard for God's kingdom throughout church history faced the same thing.

Like your Lord, you will be wounded in the house of your friends.[2]

If God's anointing is on your life and He's given you spiritual sight, the attacks that will come your way will defy human reason.

Some people will be so incited by raging jealousy that they'll work overtime to destroy your reputation in every possible way. The energy they will exert to carry this will prove so preposterous that it will baffle the most vivid imagination.

So expect conflict and use it as a springboard to turn to your Lord and rely on His good mercies.

When conflicts come, pour out your heart to Him. Consider praying Psalm 27. And always remember that the ministry you have is not yours but God's. Therefore, He can do with you as He wills. That means the conflicts, opposition, and attacks aren't your problem but, rather, His.

Remember, you're His servant, not your own (1 Corinthians 6:19-20).

T. Austin-Sparks knew about this issue all too well when he wrote,

> It is no small thing to have true spiritual sight. It represents a mighty victory. It is not going to come to you by just sitting passively and opening your mouths for it to arrive. There has to be exercise about this matter. You are right up against the full force of the god of this age when you are really out for spiritual understanding. It is a supernatural battle. So every bit of ministry that is going to be a ministry of true revelation will be surrounded by conflict. Conflict will go before, conflict will go on at the time, and conflict may follow after.[3]

David Wilkerson put it this way,

> When a man or woman of God is in the making, enemy forces will come at them with great fury. Right now you may be tasting a bitter cup of pain. You may be enduring a dark night of confusion, a terrifying hour of isolation. But I urge you to do as these men [Job, David, and Peter] did in their darkest moment, and take a stand in faith. Say as they did, "Though I be tried, and all these forces are arrayed against me, I know in whom I have believed. And I know he is able to keep that which I have committed unto him against that day."[4]

The person who is called to God's work and responds to His call has volunteered himself to hell on earth. That person will experience conflict, rejection, jealousy, misunderstanding, loneliness, and self-doubt.

But take heart! If you endure, resurrection life awaits you.

No Good Deed Goes Unpunished

I've always found the story in Matthew 8 about the two demon-possessed men to be highly ironic. The demonized men had grown so fierce that people feared to pass by the region where they lived.

Jesus entered Gentile territory and graciously delivered the two men from the demons that plagued them. The Lord ordered the evil spirits to enter a herd of two thousand pigs, who subsequently committed suicide.[5] The keepers of the pigs ran to the nearby town, telling the people what had happened.

As a result, the whole town begged Jesus to get out of Dodge and leave them alone. For them, the love of money (business) was more important than delivering humans from evil and torment.[6]

"Uh, thanks, Jesus, for casting out the demons from those two dudes. It's cool that people can now walk in these parts freely without fear. But . . . uh . . . please take off and leave us alone. We can't afford to risk losing any more businesses."

I have come to the conclusion that nothing truly good in life goes unopposed.

> Blessed are you when people insult you, persecute you and
> falsely say all kinds of evil against you because of me. Rejoice
> and be glad, because great is your reward in heaven, for in the
> same way they persecuted the prophets who were before you.
> MATTHEW 5:11-12

The patriarch Joseph was slandered, kidnapped, and then sold into slavery by his own flesh and blood. Later, he was falsely accused and thrown into prison for years.

Jealousy put Joseph in the pit and slander put him in a jail cell.

Yet because he never wavered in his trust in God, he was eventually vindicated. When the smoke cleared, God elevated Joseph to prominence, something He had promised years beforehand.

When Joseph finally met his brothers, the source of his long-term pain, he didn't exact vengeance upon them. Instead, he saw the hand of God behind it all and was able to extend forgiveness.

It's easy to resent those who have brought pain into our lives. But what if God has a deep and important purpose for allowing them to come into our lives (Romans 8:28)?

So regardless of how intense the conflicts become, take heart. Resurrection is on the other side.

But resurrection demands that you die, lay your life down, lose, and let go.

> We always carry around in our body the death of Jesus, so that
> the life of Jesus may also be revealed in our body. For we who
> are alive are always being given over to death for Jesus' sake, so
> that his life may also be revealed in our mortal body. So then,
> death is at work in us, but life is at work in you.
>
> 2 CORINTHIANS 4:10-12

The Bible says that strife (conflict and contention) is always the result of pride.

> Where there is strife, there is pride,
>   but wisdom is found in those who take advice.
>
> PROVERBS 13:10

Another translation puts it this way:

> Pride leads to conflict;
>   those who take advice are wise.
>
> PROVERBS 13:10, NLT

Dying virtually always involves the crucifixion of our pride.

But dying will mean responding differently in different situations. Here are three ways to manage conflict in Scripture. All of them include dying to self:

1. Let it go, be wronged, and forebear (Colossians 3:13; Ephesians 4:2; 1 Corinthians 6:7; Matthew 5:39).

2. Talk in private to the person with whom you have a conflict. Listen without being defensive. Correct them in a spirit of meekness, if necessary (Galatians 6:1; Matthew 18:16).

3. Find a mediator to help you resolve the conflict (1 Corinthians 6:1-6).

Each of these ways to manage conflict is biblical, but only the Holy Spirit can show you what's appropriate for a particular situation, as well as its timing.

I've learned an important lesson over the years: When in doubt, punt. That is, defer action; postpone. Let go and give the ball to the opposing team.

The Holy Spirit will sometimes lead you to delay a decision as He works the matter out behind the scenes. We often make mistakes when we rush things.

> Enthusiasm without knowledge is no good;
>   haste makes mistakes.
> PROVERBS 19:2, NLT

> The plans of the diligent lead to profit
>   as surely as haste leads to poverty.
> PROVERBS 21:5

Another point: The people to whom you minister will often go through horrible experiences. How can you minister to them if you haven't walked a similar path?

God has promised to be with us always in whatever we endure. By reading the story of Joseph in Genesis 37–50, you'll discover that God was constantly with him, through all the horrors he faced.

So long as we keep the Lord before us and stay faithful to Him, He will be with us in a special way. And from that wellspring, we can help others who suffer.

For this reason, your greatest ministry, service, and value will often come out of your greatest pain. I think Paul would agree:

> Praise be to the God and Father of our Lord Jesus Christ, the Father of compassion and the God of all comfort, who comforts us in all our troubles, so that we can comfort those in any trouble with the comfort we ourselves receive from God. For just as we share abundantly in the sufferings of Christ, so also our comfort abounds through Christ. If we are distressed, it is for your comfort and salvation; if we are comforted, it is for your comfort, which produces in you patient endurance of the same sufferings we suffer. And our hope for you is firm, because we know that just as you share in our sufferings, so also you share in our comfort.
>
> 2 CORINTHIANS 1:3-7

LAW 29

Do Not Compromise

To compromise is to lose spiritual power.

Compromise is a greased hill. If you give one inch to it early on, don't be surprised if you find yourself fully corrupted later in life.

I've been with men who had incredible ministries in their early years, only to be corrupted later because of compromise.

The peril of compromise doesn't happen overnight. It begins with the small things. A little toleration here, saying yes to a "tiny" sin there, letting your guard down, etc.

Eventually, you've lost God's anointing, which is a devastating thing to experience and a tragedy to witness. (Unfortunately, I was once given a front-row seat to the disintegration of a gifted spiritual leader. It is something I'll never forget.)

Ichabod is the final destination of those who allow compromise to seep into their lives. And compromise is one of the fastest ways to lose God's power.

What's the antidote to compromise?

Frank Laubach said it best when he wrote, "The price of spiritual power is absolute unconditional surrender to God."[1]

In a similar vein, Watchman Nee said, "God does not tolerate competition. Our all must be on the altar. This is the Christian's way to spiritual power. . . . Without the altar, there will be no heavenly fire."[2]

The secret is to keep saying yes to God, over and over again, and to say no to the world and the flesh, over and over again.

Even when it kills you.

The only way to gain spiritual power is to keep yourself squarely on the cross, no matter how often or how bad the mistreatments, injustices, criticisms, and attacks get. None of us can pull this off, even by using all the strength we can muster.

It requires—demands—that we regularly lay hold of the life of Jesus Christ.

Surrender and God's power go together like Pule cheese and fine wine, police officers and doughnuts, artsy painters and lead poisoning.

They cannot be separated.

Guard Your Heart

It only takes a few minutes of unguarded living to destroy your life. Consequently, your greatest asset in ministry is your heart, which is why Scripture exhorts us to guard it with vigilance:

> Above all else, guard your heart,
>   for everything you do flows from it.
> PROVERBS 4:23

Or as the ESV puts it: "Keep your heart with all vigilance, for from it flow the springs of life."

You must guard your heart because it's constantly under attack.

Your mind is regularly assaulted to entertain ungodly thoughts, toxic thinking patterns, and foolish temptations.

Your emotions will tempt you to allow bitterness, resentment, anger, and depression to take root.

Your conscience is always in jeopardy of being silenced and even seared.

An unhealthy heart threatens everything else in your life—not only your ministry but your family, friends, work, and health.

The Slippery Slope of Corruption

The following story has been repeated so many times it's almost predictable.

Darren was a profoundly gifted communicator who spoke eloquently, wrote compellingly, and sang impressively—a "triple threat," as the old-time preachers used to say.

In his early years as a minister, Darren vowed to never compromise his convictions. He would always tell the truth. He wouldn't drink alcohol or ever flirt with women. He also wouldn't watch R-rated movies.

As time wore on, Darren's soul become overwhelmed with discouragement. Little by little, he began to lower his guard. He began to flirt with waitresses. He'd tell "little white lies" when convenient. He even began watching films with graphic sex scenes.

Before long, Darren's soul grew so corrupted that he couldn't seem to tell truth from fiction. His lying became pervasive, even pathological. He deluded himself with false narratives. Just as alarming, his incessant flirting turned into full-blown propositions.

All of this led to enormous carnage among those close to him. Eventually, Darren lost spiritual power. Whenever he spoke, he did so without the anointing he once possessed.

Darren's life teaches us a simple lesson: Never compromise. It leads only to greater compromises, until you've chipped away so much of your spiritual fiber that little remains.

LAW 30

Equip and Empower, Do Not Control

Your job as a minister, in whatever capacity, is to work yourself out of a job. You are to bring others into the spiritual experiences that you yourself have with the Lord.

Too many ministers today have it backwards. Their work has no end game.

Their "hearers" exist to support their ministries and keep them running.

Some ministers dominate God's people by micromanaging their private lives, telling them how to vote, what to wear, whom to date, how to spend their money, how and where to educate their children, how to manage their health, etc.

They operate as overlords rather than overseers.

Authoritarian leaders like these watchdog every move of God's people, suffocating them in a blanket of control.

Contrast that with Paul's leadership:

Not that we lord it over your faith, but we work with you for your joy, because it is by faith you stand firm.

2 CORINTHIANS 1:24

The CEV renders the text this way:

We are not bosses who tell you what to believe. We are working with you to make you glad, because your faith is strong.

Or as Peter put it:

Be shepherds of God's flock . . . not lording it over those
entrusted to you, but being examples to the flock.

I PETER 5:2-3

The ESV translates the passage this way:

Shepherd the flock of God that is among you . . . not
domineering over those in your charge, but being examples
to the flock.

A genuine servant of God doesn't seek to be served by others, nor
does he want to control them.

The desire to control others, even for their own good, is fleshly.

Consequently, the Lord must break that drive in us.

Paul gives us the end game for all ministry:

To equip his people for works of service, so that the body
of Christ may be built up until we all reach unity in the
faith and in the knowledge of the Son of God and become
mature, attaining to the whole measure of the fullness of
Christ.

EPHESIANS 4:12-13

God has gifted you and me to equip the body of Christ so the
believing communities we serve can attain the fullness of Christ.

It is our adventure to find out *how* to equip and empower God's
people without controlling them.

Never Pick Up This Tool

One of the most common tools that Christian leaders wield to control
God's people is guilt.

No preacher worth his salt possesses a needle or syringe filled with something called guilt. Guilt is one of the most powerful motivators in the universe. But no servant of God ought ever to pick it up.

I can't improve upon how I put it in *Jesus Manifesto*:

> Sadly, many of us today combat problems and erroneous teachings with laws, rules, religious duty—and the mother of all religious tools: *guilt*. Some preachers need a travel agent to handle all the guilt trips they put on God's people. But there is a big difference between putting a guilt trip on Christians and unveiling Christ to them. When Christ is presented in power, the Spirit of God will undoubtedly convict those who are walking in contradiction to their new nature. But Holy Spirit conviction and man-induced guilt and condemnation are two very different things.

Paul refused to employ any of the tricks of the trade, such as guilt, fear, or strong-armed manipulation. Instead, he gave the Colossian believers a stunningly elegant vision of Christ—exalted, glorious, high and lifted up. To his mind, if he could present Christ in reality, life, and power, it would blow the false teaching to bits. All the problems in the Colossian church would fade into the background. No earthly distraction, whether true or false, could stand up to the glaring light of God's glory in the face of Jesus Christ.

To use a gambling metaphor, Paul bet on Christ and believed that He was enough to win the hearts of the Colossian Christians. Consequently, the apostle sought to put salve on the believers' eyes so they would be able to see the overwhelming greatness of their Lord. The Christ that the Colossians knew was simply too small. That was why they became susceptible to chasing other things—including religious ones—in the first place.

Sound familiar?

Paul's goal was to strip away every distraction that was being held before their eyes and leave them with nothing but

Christ. He dared to displace all rules, regulations, laws, and everything else that religion offers, with a person—the Lord Jesus Himself. As far as Paul was concerned, God hadn't sent a Ruler of the rules, a Regulator of the regulations, a Pontiff of the pontifications, or a Principal of the principles. He had sent the very embodiment of divine fullness. So, he reasoned, if the Colossians could just get a glimpse of the glories of Christ, He would be enough. The Spirit would electrify their hearts and restore them to a living relationship with the head of the body.

So Paul threw down his trump card—*the Lord Jesus Christ*. He presented a panoramic vision of Jesus that exhausts the minds of mortal men.[1]

Using guilt to motivate God's people offers a cure worse than the poison. It's putting something on God's people that Jesus set them free from!

Playing the role of a fire-breathing Moses is antithetical to Jesus Christ, who is full of grace and truth and who sets captives free with unfailing mercy and stunning grace.

For from his fullness we have all received, grace upon grace. For the law was given through Moses; grace and truth came through Jesus Christ.
JOHN 1:16-17, ESV

Similar to guilt, another tool many ministers pick up to control God's people is fear.

Not a few pastors have told ghost stories about damaged people in order to scare the liver out of those who are "out of line." It usually sounds something like this:

Unless you stay in our church, you'll become raw meat for the devil. . . . Unless you do *xyz*, something horrible is going to happen to you because you'll be out of God's will and there will be no protection. Let me tell you a few stories where tragedy befell those who left our fellowship.

Using fear to whip people into line is abhorrent. God's servants are never to be harbingers of terror to the saved. Fear is the instrument of God's enemy, so an effective minister of Jesus Christ never enters that territory.[2]

Fear brings slavery (Hebrews 2:14-15; Romans 8:15). We live under the new covenant, where we are free to serve God without fear (Luke 1:74).

The best medicine for guilt and legalism is Paul's blistering letter to the Galatians. It's a masterful treatise against legalism in all its forms.

Every Christian leader ought to be armed to the teeth with a deep understanding of this letter and know how to use it to set God's people free.[3]

Never control God's people. Equip and empower them instead.

LAW 31

Remove the Religious Mask

Ever since my teens, I've observed two different faces on many ministers. First, there's the "on" face when the minister takes the stage and gives what amounts to a religious performance.

Second, there's the "off" face, the normal one that's visible only to friends and family.

This two-faced divide is sometimes so drastic that it affects the way some ministers talk and pray, even down to the timbre of their voice.

There is the normal way they teach/preach, pray, and speak. And then there is the religious "teaching/preaching" voice, the stained-glass-window form of praying, and the "spiritual" way of speaking.

I've attended many commencement ceremonies where a reverend offered the opening prayer. We could describe these prayers as "Gothic cathedral invocations," which swing from a deep religious voice down to a bare whisper. They tend to be peppered with religious jargon such as "beseech" and "entreat" and King James–styled "Thees" and "Thous."

I'm pretty sure none of these pastors speak like this over dinner.

Just imagine: "Honey, I beseech thee to pass me the salt, and I entreat thee to hand me the pepper, too. I thankest thou."

Yeah, right.

This kind of praying is pure pretense. Staged and rehearsed. (Jesus talked about something similar, you know.)[1]

If you've ever had the displeasure of watching someone you know pray like this, you probably thought, *Who* is *this person?*

To prevent this problem, as well as to solve it, I recommend that you find out who you are and what's normal for you.

Then speak that way, preach that way, pray that way, and teach that way, whether you are "on" or "off."

Elsewhere, I've made the point that modern ministers are often taught to play a role just like a thespian in a Greek drama. Surprisingly, this "role" is bolstered by much of our theological training. But at the end of the day, it's emotionally crushing.[2]

You can pretend only for so long. And God is never impressed with our pretention.

Many young leaders try, in vain, to put on Saul's armor.[3] But if it doesn't fit, don't wear it. This includes the preachers and teachers you feel tempted to mimic.

Compliments and Exaggerations

Another area where ministers are lured to be pretentious involves exaggeration.

It's commonplace for many preachers and evangelists to puff up the numbers of those who respond to a salvation call, those who get healed, and those who attend a conference or service.

The tendency to bolster the numbers is in the drinking water of a number of current denominations and movements.

Again, the root is pretention.

Religious pretense can also rear its ugly head when someone compliments your ministry.

Some ministers respond with, "Oh, no, don't compliment me! It wasn't me. It was God" (or words to that effect).

Excuse me, but a simple "thank you" is far more appropriate as well as more human.

Feel free to follow that up with, "Praise the Lord," if it's sincere. But there's no need to turn pious in the face of a compliment.

Unfortunately, there's a certain amount of "glory" that comes with being used by God. And that glory has caused some leaders to drive off a cliff in their ministry.

So learn to treat gushing praise and unfounded criticism the same way. Plow it under as fertilizer and ignore it. Because both are posers.

If you can meet with Triumph and Disaster
  And treat those two impostors just the same . . .
You'll be a Man, my son.[4]

What helps here is to recognize—and stay in touch with—the fact that anytime people are touched by your ministry, it was God's gift. Sure, all ministry involves your labor too. But you'd be incapable of any labor without God's grace to give you health, energy, and a functioning mind.

New Testament ministry, then, is a combination of your labor fueled by God's power.

For this purpose I also labor, striving according to His power which works mightily within me.

COLOSSIANS 1:29, NASB

No paintbrush applauds itself, but being thankful for the opportunity to serve in the Painter's hands is both right and appropriate.

At the same time, declaring bulbously that it was "all God" and refusing any compliment demonstrates false humility and hyper-religiosity.

So keep your feet on the earth and resist the urge to keep the glory. Keeping the glory is the path to losing God's anointing. (Just ask King Saul.)

My challenge: Break with the two faces. Pretense, even at a subconscious level, depletes spiritual power.

Trash the religious mask and discover who you are and how you normally speak and act. This will clear the way for God's power to become an active reality in your life and service.

When the lights get bright, most people either shine or melt.

It is your task to remain normal.

LAW 32

Stay in School

I'm one of those rarified creatures who believes that a formal theological education isn't worth a whole lot when it comes to being equipped to minister the riches of Christ.[1]

I've spoken in conference after conference where some of the attendees said to me that they were angry.

The reason? They spent obscene amounts of money on a seminary education, and what they were hearing during the conference was foreign to them yet life-changing. Their response was to blow a gasket.

Many of the people to whom I minister have seminary educations. And down to the individual man or woman, virtually all of them have admitted that their seminary education didn't teach them much about the deeper things of God.

I'm sure there are exceptions (Dietrich Bonhoeffer was among them). But I'm candidly sharing my observations over three decades.

The above statements may lead some to believe that I'm against education and learning. Not so. I'm a staunch champion of learning throughout one's entire life. And I practice it myself.

Consequently, when I say, "Stay in school," I mean to keep doing your homework. Learn all you can about church history. Read the biographies of the men and women of God upon whose shoulders you stand. Keep reading. Keep studying. Keep learning, from both the living and those who have gone before us.

But don't relegate your learning to scholars and theologians. Read people like A. W. Tozer, G. Campbell Morgan, Martyn Lloyd-Jones,

Charles Spurgeon, and D. L. Moody. They all had no formal theological training.

In addition, two of the most powerful ministers of Jesus Christ—T. Austin-Sparks and Watchman Nee—never attended seminary.[2]

Furthermore, you don't have to attend seminary or Bible school to learn what scholars and theologians can offer. And you can learn from those who don't fit into those academic categories but who "know the Scriptures and the power of God" in tremendous ways.

Remember that Jesus didn't train under a priest or rabbi. He was a blue-collar worker, a working-class hero, a journeyman, a day laborer.

None of the twelve disciples had formal theological educations either. And though Paul did receive formal "religious" training, it didn't help him to know the Lord (see Philippians 3:3-14).

I'm not saying, "Stay clear of seminary." If God truly leads you there, go. My point is that it's not necessary for ministry, and it could hamper your spiritual progress.[3]

Effective Leaders Are Readers

An older Christian leader I know used to interview young men who felt called to God's work. He'd routinely ask them, "How big is your library?"

This is a great question. Why? Because effective leaders are readers.

If you aren't a reader (or at the very least, if you don't listen to audiobooks), you aren't qualified to labor in the Lord's house.

To deal with the problems of the human soul and spirit, you need to be informed on nearly everything related to human behavior as well as the spiritual realm.

The body of Christ has been with us for two thousand years. During that time, the Lord has raised up women and men with unique insight into His kingdom. And we can glean from those insights through their books.

At the end of his life, Paul requested only three things: a coat, his parchments, and his books (2 Timothy 4:13). This man knew the

Lord better than most. He wrote a large part of the New Testament, God used him to unveil His eternal purpose, and he visited the third heaven and raised up the house of God in his day.

And yet, at the end of his life, he asked for his books.

Reading a book won't make you a leader, but no good leader can neglect reading. Consider these words from Dallas Willard:

> In my early days of ministry, I spent huge amounts of time absorbed in Scripture and great spiritual writers. The Lord made it possible for me to spend whole days—without any issue of preparing for something or taking an examination—soaking up the Scripture. I literally wore out the books of great spiritual writers. This focus was foundational to my spiritual journey, to finding satisfaction in Christ.[4]

A Personal Word

If you don't like reading, take heart. I despised reading until I reached my twenties. Even now, while I don't relish the process (I'm a slow reader), I love the benefits.

I began building a library in my early twenties. A paraphrase of Erasmus described me well: "When I get a little money, I buy books; and if any is left, I buy food and clothes."[5]

However, my early purchases were hit-and-miss.

I bought discounted books, volumes whose descriptions made them sound good, as well as the "you gotta get this book!" referrals from friends.

Today, many of those books no longer appear in my library. After thumbing through the pages, I realized that I had no use for them.

Looking back, I wish I'd had some prudent guidance on the books worth buying. It would have saved me both time and money.

Since I began writing and speaking, people have asked me, "What books do you recommend I read, other than your own?"

On my blog, I've put together a list of what I consider to be the best one hundred Christian books ever written.

In my humble (but accurate) opinion, these are exceptional books—game changers.

I wish I'd had this list when I started building my own library. But today I recommend that every person who feels called to the Lord's work begin reading them.[6]

Summing up, stay in school. Because the moment you stop being a student, you stop being a teacher.

Embrace Co-Working

God built co-working into His universe. We see it all over the New Testament, from the disciples of Jesus to the men Paul trained.[1]

As followers of Jesus, we cannot escape the principle of co-laboring.

Right or wrong, I believe the greatest obstacle to the advance of the kingdom in the earth today is the unwillingness of so many of God's servants to work together. Though this isn't the case with all of them, I'd say it's true for most Christian leaders in America.

Elsewhere, I've explained the profound benefits of co-working.[2] In this chapter, I want to go for the jugular and expose two reasons why countless ministers refuse to work with others in ministry. Those reasons are jealousy and fear of diversity.

Let's unpack both.

Reason 1: Jealousy

According to music experts, the four greatest music artists of all time are Michael Jackson, Garth Brooks, the Beatles, and Led Zeppelin (those are in no particular order).

Suppose that you were a music artist performing during the prime of any of those four groups or musicians. You have a nice following, but nothing like them.

Unless you have thoroughly crucified your ego, you wouldn't want to open a show for Jackson, Brooks, the Beatles, or Zep.

Why not? Because you'd be thoroughly upstaged. They would wipe the floor with you, so you'd happily decline.

Don't think for a second this doesn't happen in Christian

conferences today. This is the reason why many of the most gifted and powerful speakers aren't invited to certain conferences.

The reason is jealousy. The unwillingness to be upstaged.

Of course, jealousy is rarely admitted. People give other excuses to cover the envy, but insecurity, rivalry, and competitiveness often lie at the root.

Consequently, it's much safer for ministers to work alone or with the less gifted.

Now imagine: What would have happened if Barnabas had refused to invite Paul to work with him in Antioch because of jealousy? Or what would have happened if all twelve apostles had refused to work with each other because of jealousy?

The kingdom of God wouldn't have moved very far.

Reason 2: Fear of Diversity

One of Watchman Nee's most brilliant books, *What Shall This Man Do?*, is an incisive study of the distinctive ministries of Peter, Paul, and John.

In the book, Nee argues that what each man was doing when Jesus called him foreshadowed their future ministries.

When Jesus called Peter, he was casting a net into the sea. Peter was fishing.

Interestingly, Peter's distinctive ministry was evangelism. He opened the door of the kingdom to both Jews and Gentiles. Jesus made him into a fisher of men.

When Jesus called Paul, he worked as a tentmaker—a builder, if you will.

Accordingly, Paul's distinctive ministry was building the house of God.

To stay with the metaphor, Peter brought in the fish, but Paul built them together into a house.

When Jesus called John, he was repairing his net. He was a restorer.

Consequently, John's distinctive ministry was restoring the house of God when it started to move toward ruin. John repaired the tent that Paul had built.

Since each man was an apostle, all three preached the gospel of the kingdom and built kingdom communities, but each had a distinctive ministry.

Peter cast the net, Paul built the house, and John repaired the net. Now here's my application.

Some movements today are made up exclusively of Peters. They emphasize nothing but reaching the lost. Each person in the movement is a Peter (even though they may mistakenly call some in the movement a Paul or a John).

Tragically, they never invite a Paul or a John into their movement, due to the fear of diversity.

To their minds, John is too radical and Paul is too intensely centered on community-building.

Peters are often jealous of Pauls because of their powerful speaking ministries. (Pauls tend to blow people's minds wherever they preach.)

The real Pauls have experience in raising up the house of God and equipping the saints to function under the headship of Christ. So their value is immense.

The real Johns are prophetic voices able to identify the root problems in the body of Christ and offer solutions. They are boat-rockers and sod-turners. So the Pauls and Johns tend to threaten the Peters.

(On occasion, God raises up someone who is a combination of the Pauline and Johannine ministries. These rare vessels cause no small ruckus.)

Not a few Christian movements are incredibly heady and intellectual, so the people invited to join arms with them are equally mindy, abstract, and intellectual.

The firebrands who minister at a deeper level get left out, along with the emoters.

Why? Fear of diversity.

If the kingdom of God is to advance today, the Peters, Pauls, and Johns must work together—but this demands something costly. It demands that the cross of Jesus Christ deal a hefty blow to the ego, demolishing its insecurities and putting to death the jealousy and fear that springs from it.

You Must Have Peers

I've watched profoundly gifted men lose a great deal of what they built because they refused to have peers.

On the one hand, they labored hard and long by employing their incredible giftings. But with their other hand, they destroyed their own work, all because they lacked peers who could speak into their lives.

Some of these men became corrupt after many years of bearing the cross, turning into Sauls.

A few of these men are still alive, and I pray for them daily, asking God to get through to their hearts so they will repent and reconcile with those who became the victims of their mad jealousy.

You can avert this tragedy in your own life. The antidote is to become intentional about having peers in your life.

Right now.

These "peers" may not be as gifted as you, they may not have your level of spiritual insight, but if you open your heart to them and allow them to speak into your life, they will become your peers.

Getting back to the point of this chapter: Lay down fear and jealousy and invite to your conference or church those with a powerful message. Lay down your fear of them outshining or upstaging you. And don't write them off just because they don't tick every theological box you subscribe to.

Thankfully, God has allowed me to have co-workers at different points in my life, men who I would go to war with and vice versa. I have gone straight to the bowels of hell for some of them, and they did the same for me.

So be willing to work with others and make sure you have peers in your life.

LAW 34

Be a Channel, Not a Pond

This law may appear to contradict Law 13, but it does not.

Law 13 (Be a Reservoir, Not a Canal) has to do with the *timing* of service. This law (Be a Channel, Not a Pond) has to do with the *nature* of service.

Frank Laubach articulated this principle well when he wrote,

> In fact, there are *two* drawbridges in the castle of our soul, and the man within has control of both. One opens *up* toward God, and the other opens *out* toward our fellow men. If we open both our drawbridges we become God's *highway*.[1]

Using another metaphor, Laubach writes,

> The pipe must be open up toward God and open down toward man. And then the currents flow through and the wheels go round and we work with the power of God. . . . Stop being a terminus and become a bridge! Stop being a bucket and become a pipe! That is the secret of receiving the power of God.[2]

According to Laubach, if some obstruction comes between us and God, the water of life will not flow out of us to others. By the same token, if some obstruction stands between us and others, the water cannot flow in or out.

The solution is to be a channel, not a pond. This requires that we vigilantly keep the channel open and without any blockage on either end, whether toward God or toward people.

What can prevent us from becoming a channel? Consider some common blockages:

- Unforgiveness (holding a grudge)
- Pride (thinking that you are better than others)
- Vainglory (vanity and the desire for praise from others)
- Oversensitivity (being thin-skinned)
- Jealousy
- A critical, faultfinding spirit
- Selfishness
- Fear (anxiety)
- Rage
- Spiritual apathy
- The pursuit of the world[3]

All these elements can kill your spiritual life.

The water of God's life is mighty and powerful, but it has to have a mission, both for us and for others.

Sometimes God seems deaf or unwilling to bless us spiritually because we've failed to look outward with a view toward serving others. On this score, Laubach writes,

> You can't have a great spiritual experience again until you have given the one you *do* have to someone else . . . because buckets cannot contain the Holy Spirit. Only pipe lines open at both ends can hold the Spirit. . . . The water of life will flow *to* us only if it flows *through* us. You can't keep it unless you give it away.[4]

Watchman Nee echoed the same thought:

> If the fountain of life within the believer ever becomes
> restrained and ceases to flow, it is not because there is
> anything wrong with the inlet; it is the outlet which has
> become obstructed. The water of life must have a way
> through. It must go somewhere. Others must enjoy it. The
> answer is simple: first clear the outlet and it will flow again
> unceasingly.[5]

Clearing the Outlet

There are two keys to becoming a channel. First, recognize that God
has called you to be an outlet as well as an inlet. Second, recognize
where the logjam lies.

Look over the list of blockages above.

Do any of these elements regularly operate in your life?

If so, deal with God over them. Fast, pray, and get someone else
to counsel you so you can repent and let them go.

Do whatever you must to clear the obstructions so the water of
life can flow in and out.

Consider these words from our Lord:

> If anyone thirsts, let him come to me and drink. Whoever
> believes in me, as the Scripture has said, "Out of his heart
> will flow rivers of living water."
>
> JOHN 7:37-38, ESV

Notice the order. First, come to Christ and drink. Second, let the
living water flow out of your heart to refresh others.

Learn to drink and experience God's living water. Then give it
away at the right time. Only as you do so will you have space for more
of God's life and power to flow in and through you.

Stay Faithful to Your Calling

One of the key ingredients to having spiritual power is to stay faithful to God. Take a close look at these two texts:

> This, then, is how you ought to regard us: as servants of Christ and as those entrusted with the mysteries God has revealed. Now it is required that those who have been given a trust must prove faithful.
>
> I CORINTHIANS 4:1-2

> Whoever can be trusted with very little can also be trusted with much, and whoever is dishonest with very little will also be dishonest with much. So if you have not been trustworthy in handling worldly wealth, who will trust you with true riches? And if you have not been trustworthy with someone else's property, who will give you property of your own?
>
> LUKE 16:10-12

God rewards faithfulness. The more faithful you are, the more He will trust you with His power.

Our main task isn't to change the world. It's not even to change people.

No, our main task is to remain faithful to the end.

The Need for Endurance

A large part of being faithful is the capacity to be resilient; that is, having the ability to endure. Life will throw all sorts of obstacles at any ministry that God values.

The servant whom the Lord uses over the long run must possess the spiritual fortitude to endure until the end.

Though the righteous fall seven times, they rise again.
PROVERBS 24:16

The guy who gets the prize is the one who breaks the tape. If, at the end of your ministry, you're still standing on your feet—"having done all, to stand"—you've endured.[1]

I have fought the good fight, I have finished the race, I have kept the faith.
2 TIMOTHY 4:7

Hold fast what you have, that no one may take your crown.
REVELATION 3:11, NKJV

Elsewhere, I have written the following about the apostolic ministry:

At the top of Paul's list of apostolic qualifications is the hallmark of spiritual power: *perseverance.*

The Greek word translated "perseverance" (and "patience" in other translations) is *hupomone.* It means the ability to abide under pressure.

It's to pass through the breaking point without being broken. It's the characteristic of a person who is not swerved from his or her purpose by even the greatest trials and sufferings.[2]

Watchman Nee elaborates,

The signs of an apostle will never be lacking where there is
truly an apostolic call. . . . Endurance is the greatest proof of
spiritual power, and it is one of the signs of an apostle. It is
the ability to endure steadfastly under continuous pressure
that tests the reality of an apostolic call.[3]

Apostles are unstoppable creatures. They can be stapled, muti-
lated, bent, stomped on, and rolled over, and yet they will get up,
and with their garments still smoking, they'll keep moving forward.

The only way to stop a genuine apostle is to kill him!

Paul's words to the Ephesian elders capture his relentless ambition to endure to the end and finish the race that God called him to
run. His words give us insight into his incredible perseverance:

I only know that in every city the Holy Spirit warns
me that prison and hardships are facing me. However,
I consider my life worth nothing to me; my only aim is
to finish the race and complete the task the Lord Jesus
has given me—the task of testifying to the good news
of God's grace.

ACTS 20:23-24

These words apply to any ministry that will bear lasting fruit.

The race is not to the swift nor to the strong. The name of the
game is endurance.

Steadfastness is critical.

Therefore, my beloved brothers, be steadfast, immovable,
always abounding in the work of the Lord, knowing that in
the Lord your labor is not in vain.

I CORINTHIANS 15:58, ESV

Let the Lord Promote You

Faithfulness is also connected to promotion.

One of the most damaging things that can be done to a person called of God is to promote them too early.

God has a "fullness of time" on His calendar, so never rush the process. Ambitious people have a difficult time with this and end up taking shortcuts that they later regret.

Paul warned Timothy to not lay hands on anyone too soon (1 Timothy 5:22). Jesus said that if we are faithful serving another, God will entrust us with that which is our own (Luke 16:10-12).

David served faithfully as a shepherd in Bethlehem before God entrusted him with the crown.

Consider the following texts that speak to this issue:

Humble yourselves, therefore, under God's mighty hand,
that he may lift you up in due time.

I PETER 5:6

Lift not up your horn on high: speak not with a stiff neck.
For promotion cometh neither from the east, nor from the west,
    nor from the south.
But God is the judge: he putteth down one, and setteth up
    another.

PSALM 75:5-7, KJV

Whoever exalts himself will be humbled, and whoever
humbles himself will be exalted.

MATTHEW 23:12, ESV

If you're young, give time for preparation and experience. Humble yourself, remain faithful in both the natural and spiritual things, and let the Lord elevate you to the next step.

If you try to take a shortcut, or you allow others to promote you prematurely, you'll do yourself and the Lord's people a monumental disservice.

I've often been asked (okay, that's not true; people rarely ask me anything, but let's pretend they did): What about the generations that come after you are gone? How do you preserve your contribution and what you've built?

One man who mentored me worked with Watchman Nee. People often asked this question of him. And here's how he answered:

> We are only responsible for what happens to our work in our generation. While we should seek to build well so that our work lasts beyond our years, it is ultimately the Lord's charge to care for what we have left behind. We aren't responsible for the generations that come after us. We are only responsible for our own.

I don't know about you, but I find this answer to be freeing.

You and I are responsible for God's work in our own generation, not beyond.

A Charge to Keep

Faithfulness, according to Scripture, touches both the natural, physical things of life as well as the supernatural, spiritual things of life. The two are connected.

As Jesus exhorted, remain faithful in the small things, be faithful with what belongs to others, and you will prove faithful in the larger things.

Make one of your goals the hearing of these words: "Well done, good and faithful servant" (Matthew 25:23).

While you may nod your head and agree with everything I just said, the difficulty comes when you face scathing criticism, the searing pain of discouragement, and the horrible sense that all the time you've invested in ministry (including countless hours of preparation) has been a colossal waste.

It is during those times that you will be tempted to be unfaithful. Whenever any of these things happen, however, you'd be wise to reread this chapter.

All told, faithfulness is critical in the Lord's work. As a minister of Christ, you've been handed a charge to keep. As Paul exhorted Timothy, so I exhort you: "Keep that which is committed to thy trust" (1 Timothy 6:20, kjv).

Let us faithfully guard the deposit that God has entrusted to us. This is yet another path to spiritual power.

Do Not Go Beyond Your Gift

According to the New Testament, God has given the body of Christ gifted individuals to carry on His work. Those gifts—or gifted members—are apostles, prophets, evangelists, and shepherds/teachers (Ephesians 4:11-12).[1]

God has also given different gifts of grace, such as encouragement, hospitality, showing mercy, and teaching (Romans 12:3-8).

In addition, there are different manifestations of the Holy Spirit, such as the word of knowledge, the word of wisdom, faith, prophetic utterances, and gifts of healing (1 Corinthians 12:7-11).

Here's the problem:

I've watched people with gifts of healing who tried to teach. And it was a disaster.

I've watched teachers try to function in the prophetic gift. And it fell to the ground.

I've watched shepherds try to carry out the apostolic ministry. And it was an epic fail.

In each case, the individuals tried to box out of their weight class, and the results weren't pretty.

Point: Stay within your calling, and don't go beyond your gifting.

An Unhealthy Obsession

Ever since I started following the Lord, I've watched Christians fret over identifying their spiritual gifts, an obsession similar to how people geek out over personality tests.

"What's your Enneagram number?"

"I'm an ISFJ on Myers-Briggs; what are you?"

"What's your DiSC personality type?"

"What did you score on the StrengthsFinder?"

A few authors have even created similar tests to determine a person's spiritual gifts.

But here's the unvarnished truth: You don't have to name your gift or even identify it to follow this crucial principle. In fact, you don't even have to "find" your gift; you "summon" it by functioning.

Therefore I remind you to stir up the gift of God which is in you through the laying on of my hands.

2 TIMOTHY 1:6, NKJV

The first time I picked up a baseball and threw it, the function felt natural to me. I didn't have to "find" or "identity" my gift of pitching beforehand. I simply did what came naturally: throw the ball, and later pitch in Little League and then high school.

In a similar way, I taught and preached long before I ever gave a single thought to my gifts. Eventually, others who watched me function made comments about my gifting.

The body of Christ knows what gifts you have, especially those believers who know you best and see you function.

You don't need a test created by a mortal to find out.

Building on Another Man's Foundation

A related word: Never seek to build on another man's foundation (Romans 15:20). Paul refused to go beyond his spiritual charge. He also never reached into another person's work (see 2 Corinthians 10:12-18).

Although this is a big subject, I'll say just a few practical words about it here.

If someone invites you to speak to a fellowship that he or she founded, go ahead and accept the invitation if you have the Lord's leading. But be careful not to cause confusion or division while there.

Apollos and Peter made this mistake when they visited Corinth. They didn't "build well" on Paul's foundation. Consequently, division ensued (see 1 Corinthians 1–3).

How does one build well when invited to speak to a fellowship he or she didn't found? I'll share my own practice.

Whenever I've been asked to speak to a church that someone else raised up, I've gone out of my way to not cause confusion.

Sometimes I begin with, "If I say anything that contradicts what [name of the person who planted the church] has taught you, then I'm wrong. And let there be no confusion."

I've also been careful not to give any practical direction unless specifically asked. If I feel I should offer some direction, I'll ask permission first.

When I get invited to build on another person's work, my role is simply to strengthen and encourage what's already been built, and nothing more.

Dividing a body of believers is a serious sin in the eyes of God. It's far worse than being doctrinally wrong. Even if you are theologically right, if you cause division in a group of believers, you're wrong.[2]

The point of all of this is to stay in your own lane. And refuse to play someone else's instrument.

Therein you will find God's power and blessing.

LAW 37

Be Quick to Apologize

An apology is a mark of humility. Ironically, Christians aren't known for making apologies. And that's regrettably true for Christian leaders as well.

Over the years, I've learned to apologize quickly.

I've apologized when I knew I was in the wrong. I've also apologized when I believed something wasn't my fault. (In such cases, I issued the apology for the sake of the other person and his or her feelings. I regard relationships to be more important than being right.)[1]

Apologizing does several things at once. It clears the conscience, restores relationship, and displays the lowliness of Christ.

Unfortunately, you can apologize so badly that you subvert your own apology.

Here are three things to avoid when you apologize:

1. Never blame the other person, even if they share some blame. A correct apology leaves the other person's "part" utterly to God.

2. Never justify or rationalize your behavior. If asked, you may offer an explanation, but make sure the explanation isn't an excuse. Self-justification is the flesh's spin doctor.

3. Never say, "I'm sorry that you [took offense, got upset, became angry, are a first-class moron]" or words to that effect. That's not an apology but an underhanded way of shifting blame.

A true apology always takes full responsibility for one's part. If the other person shares some of the blame, never bring it up while apologizing.

As Jesus said to Peter in John 21:22, "What is it to you what I do with [the other person]? You take care of your own part and follow Me" (my paraphrase).

A Tale of Two Apologies

Years ago, a friend sent me what he considered the best apology he'd ever seen. It came from a celebrity (not a Christian leader). Here it is:

> My behavior was wrong and there are no excuses. I take
> full responsibility. . . . I will work every day to regain your
> respect and trust.[2]

By contrast, here's an apology from a politician that many felt was insincere, qualifying as a non-apologetic "apology":

> To the extent anyone felt that way [uncomfortable], I am
> truly sorry about that.[3]

That's just another way of saying, "I'm sorry you were offended." There's no whiff of owning any responsibility in those words.

A better apology would have been something like this:

> I crossed a line. It was my fault. I was wrong. And I'm very
> sorry for the pain I have caused. I'm working hard on never
> making that mistake again.

Or words to that effect.

As a minister of Jesus Christ, it's your responsibility to be an example of what you want to see in God's people.

Of course, you're not perfect. No one is, and no one should expect you to be (though some very imperfect Christians will demand perfection from you).

But strive to be a model, even in your willingness to offer a genuine apology without delay whenever warranted. (Sometimes apologies aren't warranted, especially when you've already apologized. But that's another conversation.)

Walk in humility and be quick to apologize. This is another key to spiritual power.

LAW 38

Watch Your Vocabulary

From the title, you might guess I'm talking about profanity. Well, I am. Partially. But I want to address much more than that.

Cussing Christians

Let's begin by briefly discussing profanity (since you ventured a guess about it). I've known ministers who, when not in the spotlight, would cuss until the air turned blue. And for reasons that I don't understand, their consciences didn't seem fazed.

Let me be clear. You can't engage in profanity and not suffer spiritual loss. Several passages in the New Testament make God's mind clear on the matter, including two from a single book:

> Do not let any unwholesome talk come out of your mouths, but only what is helpful for building others up according to their needs, that it may benefit those who listen.
> EPHESIANS 4:29

> Nor should there be obscenity, foolish talk or coarse joking, which are out of place, but rather thanksgiving.
> EPHESIANS 5:4

Before you feel tempted to cuss me out, take a deep breath and remember that Paul wrote those words, not I.

I realize that some have tried to justify profanity with Philippians 3:8, saying that the Greek term *skubalon* is the equivalent of *sh—* today. But that's highly debatable.

Skubalon has a much broader range of meaning. According to the *Bible Dictionary of Ancient Greek*, the word means "useless" or "undesirable material subject to disposal." Refuse, garbage, excrement, manure, garbage, rubbish, swill, and scraps are all synonyms. And none are cuss words.

Others have argued that Paul allows just about everything in his statement, "Everything is permissible for me, but not all things are beneficial" (1 Corinthians 6:12, AMP).

Most scholars agree, however, that the phrase "everything is permissible" was a slogan that the Corinthians cited to justify their carnality. Paul quotes them, and then responds, "But not all things are beneficial."

A cuss word is simply an abused word that conveys a vulgar concept or image.

If you want to know what constitutes a cuss word, the answer is simple. If it can't be said on public radio or network television (without someone getting fired or reprimanded), if a teacher can't use it in the classroom without blowback, and if you don't want your small children using those terms, it's profanity.

Forsaking profanity is a basic issue in the Christian walk. The Lord often begins with His children by having them clean up their language.[1]

The way people speak reflects their culture. Our speech, therefore, ought to reflect the culture of heaven, especially since a keen connection exists between the heart and the mouth (Luke 6:45).

It's a little-known fact that people who admire you will imitate your weaknesses and eccentricities far more than your strengths.

And they'll use you as an excuse to justify their boorish behavior.

So unless you want to see all the people you've influenced have mouths as foul as Jonah Hill and Samuel L. Jackson, you'd be wise to deal with the Lord on the matter.

If you can't control your words, you have a bigger problem at stake. James directly applies a believer's lack of control over their tongue to leaders. If you can't control your tongue, he says, you can't control much else about yourself (see James 3:1-12).

But there's much more to this law than avoiding profanity.

Phrases to Watch

Many ministers use the phrase, "He came up to me," or "She came up to me," when talking about their preaching sessions.

Like it or not, this phrase communicates that you are above others. (I realize that thought may have never crossed your conscious mind, but it conveys arrogance.)

"I preached this great sermon last night, and one of the poor, miserable laymen had to climb up to me to ask their question."

Yes, the plebes must always ascend to you.

Ahem.

But why, pray tell, do people have to *come up* to you?

Yes, I know, ministers don't usually mean what I'm suggesting, but that's the image conveyed.

And how about the phrase "my people"?

"I don't think my people would go for a longer sermon. They enjoy the twenty-minute sermonettes I deliver every Sunday."

"The other day, I told my people to kick up their giving a few notches."

Excuse me—"*your* people"?

I thought they were the Lord's people.

Regardless of the motive, those words smell of dictatorship. They also communicate an ownership that's neither scriptural nor healthy.

Another phrase to remove from your vocabulary is this: "If I'm being honest," or "Let me be honest."

Those words imply that you're not always honest. If you're never dishonest, there's no need to qualify your words like this. It's like saying, "Hey, man, I'm going to be honest right now, which isn't always the case, so listen really well."

Yet another phrase to remove from your verbal lexicon is exemplified by a well-known minister whom I once heard say, "We should sometimes allow the laypeople to [such and such]."

Pardon me, but who made you lord and king? Only Jesus Christ has the right to "allow" and "prohibit" God's people with respect to action.

Also, the words *laypeople*, *layperson*, *laymen*, and *laity* should be forever evicted from your vocabulary when referring to God's people. Whatever you think about Karl Barth's theology, he was on the money when he said, "The term 'laity' is one of the worst in the vocabulary of religion and ought to be banished from the Christian conversation."[2]

Respected scholar James D. G. Dunn agreed, stating that the clergy-laity tradition has done more to undermine New Testament authority than most heresies.[3]

There's also the problem of Christianese, which I've addressed elsewhere.[4] Consider one brief example.

The universal answer to every request that a Christian doesn't want to grant is "Let me pray about it." That's usually code language for "no way!"

I'm not suggesting you shouldn't pray over opportunities and requests. But in most cases, if you're in touch with your spiritual instincts, you'll have an answer quickly.

One more thing. A negative word is twenty times more powerful than a positive word. Every positive word can melt in a day under the weight of a few negatives. I'm especially speaking of negative talk to or about another person.

A number of the churches that Paul of Tarsus planted were damaged by negative words. Consider what he wrote to the Galatians:

> But if you bite and devour one another, watch out that you
> are not consumed by one another.
>
> GALATIANS 5:15, ESV

The mouth is the part of the human body that bites. Therefore, Paul is warning against destroying one another with words.

> Death and life are in the power of the tongue,
>> And those who love it will eat its fruit.

PROVERBS 18:21, NASB

Point: Our vocabulary exposes us in a second. And it's all too possible to dig your own grave with your tongue (see James 3). If you're a leader, people are listening and observing.

So watch your vocabulary.

LAW 39

Do Not Defend Yourself

So many ministers are quick to defend themselves because they have wrapped up their identity in their ministries.

Outside of being a "pastor," "teacher," "minister," "church planter," "prophet," "reverend," "apostle," "bishop," or "archbishop," they don't know who they are.

Whenever someone criticizes or accuses them, they feel personally threatened and immediately go on the defensive.

Jesus showed us what it means to not defend ourselves. He remained consistently silent in the face of false accusation.[1]

We know that Paul defended himself once in the New Testament, but it was to a kingdom community he founded. And while doing so, he confessed that he spoke as a fool (2 Corinthians 11:17).

Paul's normal MO, however, was the same as his Lord's. He didn't defend himself.

Watchman Nee was widely known to never defend himself. When asked why, he gave this answer:

"If people trust us, there is no need to explain; if people do not trust us, there is no use in explaining."[2]

When you defend yourself, you not only display your flesh, but you rob God of the opportunity to defend you.

In addition, you look small. Defensiveness, like petulance, shrinks a person.

God's mature servants take the high road when others sling mud their way. They embrace the spirit of the Lamb.

Many years ago, a friend gave me a valuable insight. If someone splatters mud on you and you try to clean it off, you'll end up rubbing it into your body. But if you leave it alone, the sun will harden it and it will eventually flake off.

The fact is Jesus is much better at defending us than we are.

(Regrettably, when I and others have spoken against the impulse to be defensive, some people immediately think we are suggesting that a person should quietly endure physical abuse. Not so. If a crime is committed against you, go to the authorities. That is neither defensiveness nor taking vengeance.)

Reacting to Personal Attacks

Some years ago, a well-known minister was under public assault. In response, he created a video defending himself and attacking his detractors.

When I watched it, one thought repeatedly ran through my head: *Why is this behavior acceptable, especially among God's servants? Doesn't he, or anyone else, see his response as an egregious misstep?*

Jesus made His position clear on never defending oneself. He made it part of His kingdom charter:

> You have heard that it was said, "Eye for eye, and tooth for tooth." But I tell you, do not resist an evil person. If anyone slaps you on the right cheek, turn to them the other cheek also. And if anyone wants to sue you and take your shirt, hand over your coat as well. If anyone forces you to go one mile, go with them two miles. Give to the one who asks you, and do not turn away from the one who wants to borrow from you.
> MATTHEW 5:38-42

Our Lord was falsely accused, lied about, persecuted, and mistreated, yet He never responded in kind.

Strikingly, Peter exhorts us to follow Jesus' example of non-defensiveness and refusing to take revenge:

But how is it to your credit if you receive a beating for doing wrong and endure it? But if you suffer for doing good and you endure it, this is commendable before God. To this you were called, because Christ suffered for you, leaving you an example, that you should follow in his steps.

> "He committed no sin,
>   and no deceit was found in his mouth."

When they hurled their insults at him, he did not retaliate; when he suffered, he made no threats. Instead, he entrusted himself to him who judges justly.

I PETER 2:20-23

The New Testament quotes the words of the prophet Isaiah to refer to the conduct of Christ as He stood in the midst of the flamethrowers:

> He was led like a sheep to the slaughter,
>   and as a lamb before its shearer is silent,
>   so he did not open his mouth.

ACTS 8:32

Imagine how excruciating it must have been for the Lord to pull off that feat. He stood before fallen, corrupt mortals who tried Him unfairly. Watch Him standing among them, listening to their verbal abuse, their blasphemy, their false accusations.

And He never utters a word.

The conduct of divine life is to remain silent in the face of accusation.

When you come under attack, everything in you wants to give an answer—but that's your flesh. And in most cases, to say anything is to put a noose around your neck.

Defending others is a different story. But to defend ourselves when under assault is to smack against the cross of Christ.

The cross is shock therapy for a world addicted to solving its problems through violence and the counterpunch.

Consider these timeless words by A. W. Tozer:

> In the kingdom of God, the surest way to lose something
> is to try to protect it, and the best way to keep it is to let
> it go. The law of keeping by surrendering and losing by
> defending is revealed by our Lord in His celebrated but little
> understood declaration: "If any man will come after me,
> let him deny himself, and take up his cross, and follow me"
> (Matthew 16:24).[3]

Leave Your Reputation to the Lord

As a servant of God, it's impossible to have an unassailable reputation. That's one of the first things to leave at the door when you put your hand to the plow of God's work.

A great number of men and women will kill to preserve and protect their reputations, but Jesus repeatedly told us to "lose" our lives.

Perhaps the greatest form of losing is the willingness to put our reputations in God's hands, especially when others are expending every metabolic calorie trying to destroy it.

Consider your Lord, the premium example for you, me, and all who labor for God. Ponder the long list of misrepresentations and false accusations leveled against Jesus during His earthly days. People accused Him of being:

- an illegitimate child (John 8:41)
- a deceiver (John 7:12)
- mentally ill (John 10:20)
- demon possessed (Matthew 9:34; John 7:20)
- Beelzebub [Satan] (Matthew 10:25)
- a blasphemer (Matthew 9:3; 26:65; Mark 2:7; Luke 5:21)
- a law-breaker ["unbiblical"] (Mark 2:24; Luke 13:14)

- a false prophet (Luke 7:39)
- a glutton (Matthew 11:19)
- a drunkard (Matthew 11:19)

His opponents also accused Him of saying that He would destroy the Temple in Jerusalem (Mark 14:58).

At best, Jesus' words were misunderstood by His own followers (John 21:22-23). At worst, they were deliberately twisted by His detractors (Matthew 26:60-61).

In addition, Jesus was betrayed by one of His disciples, denied by one of His closest followers, and, in His darkest hour, deserted by all of them. (To their credit, His female disciples never left Him.)

Interestingly, Jesus said these striking words to His followers:

Remember what I told you: "A servant is not greater than his master." If they persecuted me, they will persecute you also. If they obeyed my teaching, they will obey yours also.
JOHN 15:20

It is enough for students to be like their teachers, and servants like their masters. If the head of the house has been called Beelzebul, how much more the members of his household!
MATTHEW 10:25

These words were fulfilled in a disciple named Paul of Tarsus. Paul's contemporaries consistently spread slander about him.

These opponents accused Paul of

- being a man pleaser and a coward (Galatians 1:10; 1 Thessalonians 2:4)
- being a false apostle (Galatians 1:11–2:10; 2 Corinthians 11:16–12:12)

- being a flatterer (1 Thessalonians 2:5)
- being greedy (1 Thessalonians 2:5, 9)
- seeking glory from men (1 Thessalonians 2:6)
- extorting God's people (2 Corinthians 2:17; 11:7-9)
- being a deceiver and a crafty manipulator (2 Corinthians 6:8; 12:16)
- being a controller (2 Corinthians 10:1-2, 9-11)
- blasphemy (Acts 24:6)
- being a "cult" leader (Acts 24:5)
- being a criminal (Acts 16:20-21; 24:5; 2 Timothy 2:9)

People insulted Paul (2 Corinthians 12:10), gave him a bad report (2 Corinthians 6:8), and sought to destroy his reputation. Also, his good was spoken of as evil (1 Corinthians 10:30; Romans 14:16).

King David suffered in similar ways centuries before. When David landed in some trouble, a man named Shimei launched a smear campaign against him.

In the face of relentless false accusations, one of David's servants told the king, "Just say the word, and I'll remove this smear merchant's head from his shoulders. And he won't be able to slander you again" (2 Samuel 16:9, my paraphrase).

What did David do? He took the highest road possible. He replied,

Leave him alone; let him curse, for the LORD has told him to. It may be that the LORD will look upon my misery and restore to me his covenant blessing instead of his curse today.
2 SAMUEL 16:11-12

Notice the following:

1. *David recognized God's sovereignty.* He knew that the Lord stood behind the curtain, permitting Shimei to smear him.
2. *David refused to defend himself.* Instead, he put the matter fully in God's hands.

Follow the path of David and give your reputation to God. And then keep it in His capable hands.

When God Vindicates

Henry Suso, a saintly man and a bachelor, lived in the fourth century in Germany. He regularly prayed that the Lord would break him, making him humble like Christ.

One day, Suso heard someone knocking on his door. When he opened it, he saw a female stranger with a baby in her arms.

According to the story, the woman yelled, "Here is the fruit of your sin." She then transferred the baby to Suso's arms and left.

Suso was shocked and mortified, but he took the baby into his home and knelt down to pray: "Lord, you know I'm innocent. What must I do now?"

The Lord replied, "Do what I did. Suffer for the sins of others."

Suso's reputation was horribly tarnished, yet he never defended himself. Instead, he raised the child as his own. He knew what was true and false and left the misunderstandings, the harsh criticisms, the judgments, and the false accusations with the Lord.

Years later, the woman who had left the infant with Suso returned to his home and told all his neighbors that she had lied. The child was not Suso's.

Suso believed that God had answered his prayers to be broken and to impart the humility of Christ into his soul.

Though an unbeliever incited Suso's crisis, the chief attacks you will face as a minister of God's Word will come from fellow ministers. Read church history and you'll be awed at how much blood has been spilled at the hands of Christian leaders.

Blindsided and Ambushed

A long time ago, I watched as a Christian worker was blindsided and ambushed by a group of five ministers. It was a full-frontal attack. For over an hour, the men hurled accusations against him, all of which were blatantly false or grossly exaggerated.

They verbally roasted the worker over a slow spit, cut him to ribbons, scalped him, skinned him alive, and ripped him to shreds. Then, for good measure, they decapitated and steamrolled him. After that, they scolded, excoriated, impugned, rebuked, belittled, embarrassed, derided, and insulted him under a hail of criticism.

All the while, the worker never breathed a word. He kept quiet.

When it ended, the room fell silent. The worker finally opened his mouth and said one thing. He asked the men to pray for him.

It was a moment not to be forgotten.

Within weeks after the meeting, the man who orchestrated the verbal lynching (and brought the rope) had a stroke. And the lives of some of the other men began to fall apart.

Lesson: When under attack, never defend yourself. Let the Lord defend you. He'll always do a better job of it.

If you're making a spiritual impact, some people will get their knives out for you and will assault your reputation. How you respond will reveal volumes about your spiritual stature.

Resolve to become like the Man who had "no reputation" (Philippians 2:7, KJV). And remember His words:

Woe to you when everyone speaks well of you,
for that is how their ancestors treated the false prophets.

LUKE 6:26

On that point, I personally don't trust any leader who has no enemies.

Finally, there's a big difference between defending yourself and answering a question. For example, if someone has the integrity to come to you and ask, "I heard you kick cute puppies in dark alleys; is that true?" you aren't defending yourself if you respond.

Why? Because you were specifically asked.

But going nose-to-nose with those who spew venom isn't the Lord's way. If you engage in it, you'll lose spiritual power.

LAW 40

Remain Poor in Spirit

The poor in spirit receive the riches of Christ, including God's power.

Jesus' sobering words to the Laodicean church contain a stern rebuke against the opposite, being rich in spirit:

> You say, "I am rich; I have acquired wealth and do not need a thing." But you do not realize that you are wretched, pitiful, poor, blind and naked. I counsel you to buy from me gold refined in the fire, so you can become rich; and white clothes to wear, so you can cover your shameful nakedness; and salve to put on your eyes, so you can see.
>
> REVELATION 3:17-18

The Pharisees were rich in spirit. So were the Scribes and Sadducees. That's why all three groups failed to recognize the living God when He walked right under their noses.

> The people of Jerusalem and their rulers did not recognize Jesus, yet in condemning him they fulfilled the words of the prophets that are read every Sabbath.
>
> ACTS 13:27

This text shows us that it's possible to read and even memorize Scripture and yet miss the speaking of God.[1]

The genuine servant of the Lord appears confident in front of others, but within himself, he trembles in fear.

188 || 48 LAWS OF SPIRITUAL POWER

Not trusting his gifts, natural charisma, or talents, he feels a sense of inadequacy when handling spiritual things.

The Lord's servant appears bold before mortals, but on the inside, she has no confidence in her abilities. She places her confidence squarely on the Lord.

Fully Dependent

In His famous message about life in the kingdom of God, Jesus said,

> Blessed are the poor in spirit,
> for theirs is the kingdom of heaven.
>
> MATTHEW 5:3

The Amplified Bible renders the verse this way:

> Blessed [spiritually prosperous, happy, to be admired] are the poor in spirit [those devoid of spiritual arrogance, those who regard themselves as insignificant], for theirs is the kingdom of heaven [both now and forever].

I particularly like how the God's Word Translation puts it:

> Blessed are those who recognize they are spiritually helpless. The kingdom of heaven belongs to them.

To be poor in spirit is to have the heart of a helpless, dependent child. The testimony of Scripture is united on how vital this posture is to God.

> But Jesus called the children to him and said, "Let the little children come to me, and do not hinder them, for the kingdom of God belongs to such as these."
>
> LUKE 18:16

And he said: "Truly I tell you, unless you change and become like little children, you will never enter the kingdom of heaven."
MATTHEW 18:3

At that time Jesus said, "I praise you, Father, Lord of heaven and earth, because you have hidden these things from the wise and learned, and revealed them to little children."
MATTHEW 11:25

But God chose the foolish things of the world to shame the wise; God chose the weak things of the world to shame the strong. God chose the lowly things of this world and the despised things—and the things that are not—to nullify the things that are, so that no one may boast before him.
I CORINTHIANS 1:27-29

I'm inclined to agree with Kenneth Bailey in thinking that Jesus probably borrowed the phrase "poor in spirit" from Isaiah.[2]

"For all those things My hand has made,
And all those things exist,"
Says the LORD.
"But on this one will I look:
On him who is poor and of a contrite spirit,
And who trembles at My word."
ISAIAH 66:2, NKJV[3]

To be poor in spirit is to lower oneself like an open-hearted, curious student, humble enough to learn from others.

Jesus embodied being poor in spirit. Even though He possessed the full gamut of spiritual gifts, Paul tells us that He "emptied Himself" (ESV) or "made himself nothing" (NIV).

Have this mind among yourselves, which is yours in Christ
Jesus, who, though he was in the form of God, did not
count equality with God a thing to be grasped, but emptied
himself, by taking the form of a servant, being born in
the likeness of men. And being found in human form, he
humbled himself.

PHILIPPIANS 2:5-8, ESV

Being poor in spirit means making room in your life for God and
His power to fill it. In fact, we cannot know the fullness of Christ until
we are emptied of everything else and then maintain that posture.

It's possible to start your Christian life by being poor in spirit, only
to allow pride to grip your heart down the road.

Knowledge inflates with pride.

I CORINTHIANS 8:1, HCSB

Do you see a man who is wise in his own eyes? There is more
hope for a fool than for him.

PROVERBS 26:12, ESV

The Community of the Desperate

Being poverty-stricken in spirit means having childlike helplessness.
But it also includes an attitude of desperation for God.

The degree to which you are desperate to know the Lord in the
depths, to understand His ways, and to be like Him, is the degree to
which He will respond to your heart's desire.

Blind, pure, unvarnished desperation ought to be our default.

One purpose of trials and tribulations is to keep us desperate for
God. Getting put in the crucible of crisis has a way of making us poor
in spirit.

Rightly conceived, a genuine ekklesia—a kingdom community—
is the kinship of the desperate.

Here's how I put it in *Jesus Speaks*:

Jesus drove a standard in the ground when He said that the kingdom of the heavens (the unseen, heavenly realm where Christ rules) belongs to the poor in spirit. Hearing the voice of Jesus is part of that other realm.

Being poor in spirit, then, means having a childlike humility and a poverty-stricken desperation for the Lord.[4]

Jesus Himself showed us what being poor in spirit was all about.

Each day He lived on this earth, Jesus lived in constant desperation and neediness for His Father. He indicated this when He said, "I can do nothing on my own" (John 5:30, NLT).

Later on, He said to you and me, "Apart from me you can do nothing" (John 15:5).

Do you want to hear the Lord speak and keep speaking? Do you want God's power for life and service?

Become poor in spirit. And stay poor in spirit.

No matter how much the Lord shows you and does through you, it's vital that you remain desperate for Him. Helpless and needy.

Why? Because the day you stop being desperate for your Lord is the day you become rich in spirit.

And this will mute your ears to the voice of Christ as well as cause you to lose His power.[5]

Poverty of spirit is the gateway to receiving God's power. Richness in spirit forfeits the Lord's anointing because it leaves little room for Him.

Remain poor in spirit, because the richness, power, and glory of God's kingdom belong to the spiritually helpless.

Rethink Success

Instead of overselling you a vision for success, I want to help you rethink your definition of success.

Success according to God's dictionary differs drastically from success in the world.

Unfortunately, much of American Christianity today has adopted the standards of the world when it comes to defining and measuring success.

And so have many spiritual leaders.

The pursuit of success is often the impulse that drives spending big money on a theological education in the hopes of larger incomes, more speaking gigs, more wealth, bigger numbers, etc.

But God's view of success is quite different. Consider:

Brothers and sisters, think of what you were when you were called. Not many of you were wise by human standards; not many were influential; not many were of noble birth. But God chose the foolish things of the world to shame the wise; God chose the weak things of the world to shame the strong. God chose the lowly things of this world and the despised things—and the things that are not—to nullify the things that are, so that no one may boast before him. It is because of him that you are in Christ Jesus, who has become for us wisdom from God—that is, our righteousness, holiness and redemption. Therefore, as it is written: "Let the one who boasts boast in the Lord."

1 CORINTHIANS 1:26-31

The Lord's measure of success focuses on quality and longevity (staying power), not the outward marks of attendance, buildings, and cash (what Dallas Willard called "the ABCs" of modern Christianity).

Check out these timeless words:

> For no other foundation can anyone lay than that which is laid, which is Jesus Christ. Now if anyone builds on this foundation with gold, silver, precious stones, wood, hay, straw, each one's work will become clear; for the Day will declare it, because it will be revealed by fire; and the fire will test each one's work, of what sort it is. If anyone's work which he has built on it endures, he will receive a reward. If anyone's work is burned, he will suffer loss; but he himself will be saved, yet so as through fire.
>
> 1 CORINTHIANS 3:11-15, NKJV

Paul was interested in quality more than quantity. He was more concerned with what the house was built with than with its size.

If it wasn't assembled with "gold, silver, precious stones," it wouldn't stand the test of time.

What determines the success, longevity, and quality of a ministry is not any human technique or method. The cutting edge must be Jesus Christ as the only foundation, the centrality, the supremacy, the motivation, and the goal.

I am keenly aware that virtually every Christian happily claims that Jesus is "the center" and reason for what they're doing. But listen to their rhetoric carefully, and you'll discover if it's Christ or some other thing that's being pushed or promoted.

Dancing with Fear

We who serve the Lord must learn to dance with the fear of failure. Surprisingly, fear is often a signal that we are moving toward God's will.

An oft-repeated quote is, "Don't be afraid to go out on a limb, because that's where the fruit is."

Have you failed in your ministry? You're not alone. You're not abnormal. You're not a hopeless case.

In fact, to experience failure in ministry is healthy because it produces invaluable lessons like humility and God-reliance (as opposed to self-reliance).

But that's not all.

In God's upside-down kingdom, our failures often mean the Lord's successes. How? Because it is in our weakness that we find His strength. And it is in our failures that we find His triumph.

God works in human frailty. His power is demonstrated in weakness.[1]

Put another way, if I minister in order to be "successful," then God is not winning. But if I'm prepared to fail, I not only dispel my fears, but I unlock the door for the Lord to succeed.

Because failure produces humility, I don't trust any leader who hasn't failed in some way in his or her ministry.

Failure produces meekness. It breeds brokenness. And these elements open the way for Christ to be glorified in and through us.

My own metric for success is this: Did I act or react according to my core values?[2]

If I did, then I regard it as a success in the kingdom of God, no matter the outcome.

A Word about Reassurance

Reassurance doesn't scale, which means we can never get enough of it. At the bottom of the quest for reassurance is the desire to know that our future is going to be okay.

But no human can predict the future. Looking for external

validation, therefore, undermines our trust in God and in the abilities He's given us.

Welcome confirmation and positive feedback, but refuse to seek reassurance. And never believe that you need it.

Those who succeed in God's work and steward His power well seek to please their Lord regardless of outcomes. This is another key to spiritual power.

LAW 42

Pay Attention

Not a few churches have fallen apart because those laboring among them lacked the eyes of a shepherd.

In other words, these individuals failed to pay attention, so they missed the seeds of the church's own destruction, even as those seeds were sprouting before their eyes.

The leaders I have in mind chased down all the splashes while ignoring the fountain that produced them. They could play checkers but not chess. That is, they couldn't see around corners.

All things in this world tend toward entropy, even in the body of Christ. Consequently, those who labor in the Lord must constantly give attention to the panoramic needs of God's people.

Effective ministers must possess keen powers of observation and the ability to navigate land mines. They need to be able to discern what's happening in the natural realm as well as in the spiritual realm.

I believe this skill can be developed and honed. But it begins with becoming aware of the enormous importance of observation.

Without it, you may see your labor in the Lord overturned unnecessarily.

Co-working with another servant of God can aid with this. What may escape your notice, your co-worker might spot, provided that your co-worker has eyes to see. (Two oblivious co-workers are no help.)

A Case Study

Jeff had a ministry of planting microchurches. He had a good understanding of God's purpose and the centrality of Christ.

He traveled often, responding to requests to visit sprouting fellowships and teaching them how to meet in a simple, informal way.

Sometimes Jeff would spend months with these groups, seeking to give them a strong foundation.

Tragically, however, more than 90 percent of the groups Jeff worked with dissolved within two years after he left them. The reason? It had nothing to do with the type of local churches he founded. The problem was that he lacked the necessary powers of observation. He did not see the "seeds" of destruction that had emerged.

Consequently, once Jeff left these groups, those seeds began to sprout rapidly until they choked out the life of the fellowships.

Spiritual power is pretty useless if you can't discern or see those things that will thwart its results.

If you will put your hand to the plow of God's work, therefore, it's mission critical, essential, vitally important, massively significant, and profoundly imperative to never *ever* neglect the importance of paying attention.

If you lack in this area, find someone to work with you who has this skill. See Law 33 (Embrace Co-Working).

Two Other Aspects

The aspect of paying attention I've been focusing on has to do with the ability to look outside a windshield. That is, the ability to observe what's going on around you and among the people and groups to whom you minister.

Another aspect of paying attention is the ability to look into a bathroom mirror. That is, to be self-aware. Without self-awareness, you're doomed to hamper your own transformation.

Still a third aspect of paying attention is to possess a rearview mirror. That is, to recognize the mistakes you've made in the past and correct your course.

Ministers who lack a rearview mirror end up repeating the same errors over and over. Ministers with no self-awareness never change for the better. And ministers who can't look out of windshields will watch the destruction of their labor in the Lord.

All of these skills take practice.

A good beginning is to start journaling your observations about yourself and others. And then invite those closest to you to openly share their observations with you.

Stay alert. And learn the art of becoming acutely aware.

LAW 43

Speak to the Heart

In my observation, most preachers and teachers today speak to the intellect. Their talks swell the cranium.

Others speak to the emotions. Their messages are filled with blood and thunder.

But the heart is deeper than both. And as a minister of God's Word, it's vital that you know how to engage the hearts of your listeners.

By "heart," I mean the human spirit, about which the New Testament speaks a great deal.[1]

> Let it be the hidden person of the heart . . . a gentle and
> quiet spirit.
> 1 PETER 3:4, NKJV

Many Christians confuse intellectual, academic knowledge with spiritual knowledge and insight. But the two are not the same.

Academic knowledge doesn't get past the frontal lobe, while spiritual knowledge ministers life.

Jesus taught His disciples very little theology. Have you noticed that? He mostly spoke about character transformation, knowing God, the nature of God's kingdom, and following the King (Himself).

You can know the Bible and not know God. I offer you Exhibits A, B, C, and D: the Pharisees, Sadducees, scribes, and elders in Jerusalem during Jesus' day.

These men knew more about theology than God does!

Their knowledge of the Scriptures far exceeded that of most scholars today, yet they didn't recognize the living God when He stood right in front of them.

Interestingly, Jesus said that even though the Sadducees intellectually grasped the Scriptures, they didn't understand them. Nor did they know God's power.

> But Jesus answered and said to them, "You are mistaken, since you do not understand the Scriptures nor the power of God."
> MATTHEW 22:29, NASB

It's possible to get an A in Bible study but flunk Jesus.

Unfortunately, many ministers today only wield the tools of intellectual knowledge and willpower.

But these tools are inadequate. Using them in God's work is like trying to dig a canal with a plastic spoon.

Nicodemus is not alone in the number of religious leaders, professors, and teachers who disseminate the things of God to the left or the right brain.[2] But the human spirit—the heart—transcends both.

The human spirit is the deepest part of us. The Bible calls it "the lamp of the LORD" (Proverbs 20:27). It's the dwelling place of God's Spirit.

The person who ministers to the mind, using heady concepts, lofty language, ponderous ideas, and philosophical jargon, operates on a completely different plane than the one who speaks by the Spirit of God and ministers to "the hidden person of the heart."

One disseminates ideas; the other dispenses Christ.

An individual with a natural bent toward intellectual things will quickly gravitate toward teachers and preachers who operate from the frontal lobe, wrongly equating academic knowledge with spiritual life and insight.

Life vs. Truth

Old covenant preaching was marked by dispensing information; new covenant preaching is marked by dispensing life. (See 2 Corinthians 3 for the contrast.)

There's a tremendous difference between sharing truthful information and ministering life.

A person ministering life will speak truth, but a person can speak truth without life.

When the latter happens, one's words become sterile, wooden, and dead, even though they may be biblically sound and mentally stimulating.

The letter of the law is true, but without the Spirit's anointing, it's dead.

> For the letter kills, but the Spirit gives life.
> 2 CORINTHIANS 3:6, NKJV

A wonderful story from the life of Watchman Nee tells how when he was a young man, Nee found a mentor in a missionary named Margaret Barber.

Whenever someone new came to town to preach, Nee would take Barber to the meeting to hear the new preacher. Nee would say, "You've got to hear this man. He's a great preacher; come and listen." So she did.

After it ended, Barber would say, "That man has a lot of knowledge. But he doesn't have a living experience with Christ, and he didn't minister life." This happened repeatedly.

Eventually, Nee developed his spiritual senses to the point where he also could discern between head knowledge and life.

In 1 Corinthians 1:20–2:16, Paul lays out the difference between head knowledge (academic understanding) and spiritual knowledge (revelation or spiritual insight).

I won't quote the passage here because of its length, but I suggest you read it when you finish this chapter.

Two Preachers

To minister in the power of God is to speak to the human heart. Consider Paul's words:

> For the kingdom of God does not consist in talk but in
> power.
> I CORINTHIANS 4:20, ESV

Imagine two preachers. They both deliver the same message. Every word is biblically accurate and sound.

When Jake delivers the message, it comes with power. It sways people's hearts, and they sense the life of God coming through his words. The Spirit inspires and enlightens some, challenges and encourages others.

Something has happened in the hearts of those who hear Jake.

Rick preaches the same message, verbatim. But his words fall flat. The message has no life, no power, and no influence.

How can this be?

Because Jake ministered under the anointing of the Spirit, while Rick relied on the energy of the flesh. Paul explains:

> For our gospel came to you not with mere words but also
> with power and with the holy Spirit, with ample conviction
> on our part.
> I THESSALONIANS 1:5, MOF

Jake spoke straight to the heart, while Rick spoke to the mind or the emotions.

Speaking to the intellect won't get past the hearer's memory (or notebook, which usually ends up collecting dust in a drawer or bookshelf).

Speaking to the emotions will last only so long as the emotional experience continues.

But speaking to the heart produces transformation.

Ministering to the human spirit empowers as well as educates.

No one can speak to the hearts of people, however, until one's own heart has first been touched.

Brennan Manning gave me one of the best pieces of advice I ever received. When we spoke at a conference together, I pulled him aside and asked him,

"What's the best piece of writing advice you can give me?"

I'll never forget his response.

"If it doesn't move you," he said, "throw it in the trash. Because it won't move anyone else."

The same principle applies to spoken ministry.

One of the keys to speaking with God's power is to have your own heart moved by the Lord. Only then will it give life to others.

No Eye Has Seen nor Ear Heard

Consider these words by Paul:

That is what the Scriptures mean when they say,

"No eye has seen, no ear has heard,
    and no mind has imagined
what God has prepared
    for those who love him."

But it was to us that God revealed these things by his Spirit. For his Spirit searches out everything and shows us God's deep secrets.

1 CORINTHIANS 2:9-10, NLT

So don't boast about following a particular human leader. For everything belongs to you—whether Paul or Apollos or

Peter, or the world, or life and death, or the present and the future. Everything belongs to you, and you belong to Christ, and Christ belongs to God.

1 CORINTHIANS 3:21-23, NLT

As a young Christian, I often heard preachers quote 1 Corinthians 2:9, explaining that heaven will be wonderful. No eye has seen it, no ear has heard it, and the mind cannot conceive it.

I'm sure they're right—although the destination of heaven is earth, where the two will be joined together as they were in the Garden of Eden. But that's another topic.

I did not see at the time, however, that Paul's rough quote of Isaiah 64:4 fit the situation in Corinth perfectly.

The first three chapters of 1 Corinthians indicate that Peter and Apollos visited Corinth in Paul's absence.

Apollos had become known for his great orations and knowledge of the Scriptures (Acts 18:24).

He thrilled the ear.

Peter had become known for performing great signs and wonders.

He excited the eye.

When the two men left, the Corinthian assembly began fracturing over their favorite apostle.

Some said, "We are of Peter"—these were the miracle-seekers in the fellowship, no doubt Jewish believers. As Paul put it in 1 Corinthians 1, they chased power.

Others said, "We are of Apollos"—these were the knowledge-seekers in the fellowship, no doubt Greek believers. As Paul put it in 1 Corinthians 1, they chased wisdom.[3]

Paul dwarfed both interests by saying that Jesus Christ is God's power and God's wisdom:

For Jews demand signs and Greeks seek wisdom, but we preach Christ crucified, a stumbling block to Jews and folly

to Gentiles, but to those who are called, both Jews and
Greeks, Christ the power of God and the wisdom of God.

I CORINTHIANS 1:22-24, ESV

What counts is not the eye that sees miracles, signs, wonders, and
outward power. Nor is it the ear that hears eloquence, knowledge,
and wisdom.

What counts is what the Spirit reveals. And the Spirit reveals Jesus
Christ—the power and wisdom of God!

Two Common Questions

Preachers often commonly ask two questions on this topic.

Question 1: *I preach regularly. But recently, I've been going through
hell on earth and am having a hard time ministering. Do you have any
advice?*

There have been times when I've been speaking at a conference
and I received horrible news. It was so bad it troubled my soul beyond
measure. But an older leader taught me something powerful many
years ago.

When people rain damnation on you or a death knell rings
over your life, that's often when you will bring your most powerful
messages.

Tell yourself that you must declare something higher than how
you feel. That's the secret. And lean extra hard on the Lord.

Question 2: *Sometimes as I prepare a message, I feel guilty because I
remember a sin I committed. Maybe I got into a domestic wrangle with
my wife and kids and now I feel horrible. This sometimes happens right
before I speak. I feel I'm unworthy to minister. How do I get past this?*

Ask yourself, "Am I more worthy when I haven't sinned than when
I have?"

If you believe your worthiness is tied to your obedience and conduct, then you have based it on your work rather than on the Lord's.

Only the shed blood of Christ makes us worthy before God.

Remember, when God called you, He factored in all the bone-headed mistakes you'd make, and that didn't alter His calling.

Penetrate the veil of guilt by standing by faith in the shed blood of Christ. That blood cleanses us from all sin. Confession can certainly help with this, as does faith in the atonement of Christ on your behalf.

> If we confess our sins, he is faithful and just and will forgive us our sins and purify us from all unrighteousness. . . . My dear children, I write this to you so that you will not sin. But if anybody does sin, we have an advocate with the Father— Jesus Christ, the Righteous One. He is the atoning sacrifice for our sins, and not only for ours but also for the sins of the whole world.
>
> I JOHN I:9; 2:I-2

Take a quick pause and read 1 Corinthians 1:20–2:26 in your favorite translation. Note the impressive difference Paul draws between head knowledge and true spiritual insight.

Never Waste a Trial

My book *Hang On, Let Go* is a trench-tested field guide on how not to waste your trials, tribulations, and sufferings.

In this chapter, I would like to add to some of the points I made in that book.

Suffering is both the virtue and the vice of serving God. The more gifted you are, the more heat will get turned up in your life.

The sufferings we experience are meant to break us so that God's light can gain further ground in our hearts and seep through to others. Allow me to riff on brokenness for a moment.

Brokenness

In my experience, most ministers do not understand brokenness, and those who do tend to underestimate it.

The darkest days I've ever lived were leveraged by God to break me. Why? So that the light of Christ could penetrate more deeply.

Everyone chosen for the Lord's work knows that it has been a slow, burning hell for God to take whatever ground He's taken. This transformational work in our souls requires continuous adversity.

You'll find yourself emerging out of the ashes only to meet the next shipment of nails arriving at your door. Thankfully, you do get some pauses between hurricanes.

The incessant arguments about how good and evil work in God's world have been debated endlessly. I'm not going to get into the theological weeds in this chapter, but you can see how I've sorted it out elsewhere.[1]

If God has His hand on your life, crucifixion awaits you. (I understand that this concept is alien to many contemporary readers.)

Brace yourself for the next section.

It very well may mean years of unmitigated torture. You'll scream all the way to the funeral. You may even come dangerously close to choosing Hades rather than have the suffering continue.

However, God can't break you until you've first given Him permission to do so.

The breaking hand of God is necessary for His kingdom to move forward. Suffering transforms. We find the treasure in the trials. We get our highest education in the university of adversity.

In ministry, if you don't have passion, you have nothing. And it takes a certain measure of breaking in our lives to sustain passion.

If you can pass through all the pressures that God allows into your life—the cares of this world, the drama of other people, wall-to-wall criticism, unjust treatment, crises that would kill an elephant—and still be breathing fire for God, then you just may be called to His work.

Watchman Nee rightly observed:

> Wherever there is pressure there is also power. . . . Only those who have experienced being weighed down under pressure know what power is. The greater the pressure the more power. . . . When you encounter many pressures, you should ever remember that pressure is power, and therefore you must not avoid such pressures, but welcome them. For the greater your pressure is, the greater will be your power. You will overcome all and attain to greater strength.[2]

Nee based his observation on this important text:

> We do not want you to be uninformed, brothers and sisters, about the troubles we experienced in the province of Asia. We were under great pressure, far beyond our ability to endure, so that we despaired of life itself. Indeed, we felt we

had received the sentence of death. But this happened that
we might not rely on ourselves but on God, who raises the
dead. He has delivered us from such a deadly peril, and he
will deliver us again. On him we have set our hope that he
will continue to deliver us.

2 CORINTHIANS 1:8-10

The Scriptures talk a great deal about the positive side of trials
and tribulations.

According to the New Testament, the pressure that comes from
trials develops character. Suffering produces patience. Persecution and
failure give birth to humility. Adversity produces strength and endurance. Loss creates appreciation for what God has given.

That is, if you don't waste your trials.

Let me pass on a piece of wisdom. Whenever you undergo a new
trial, ask yourself, "What new opportunities does this trial make possible for me?"

Every trial represents an opportunity to discover a fresh aspect of
Jesus Christ and watch Him change your character.

That is why, for Christ's sake, I delight in weaknesses, in
insults, in hardships, in persecutions, in difficulties. For
when I am weak, then I am strong.

2 CORINTHIANS 12:10

Indeed, there is transformative power in suffering when it's sub-
mitted to God. And it takes a lot more to break a man or a woman
than we might realize.

Consequently, servants of the Lord must learn to lean into their
trials instead of running from them.

Endure suffering along with me, as a good soldier of Christ
Jesus.

2 TIMOTHY 2:3, NLT

Every person called to ministry must have a rendezvous with God over this issue of suffering and brokenness.

How you view your trials will set your attitude toward them, and this will ultimately determine how much mileage the Lord can gain in your life.

The Marks of an Unbroken Vessel

To put a finer point on it, the evidences of an unbroken vessel are as follows:

- Defensiveness
- Justifying
- Rationalizing
- Making excuses
- Unwillingness to admit one is wrong
- Inability to receive correction
- Refusing to apologize
- Laying blame at the feet of others or God

The unbroken soul also has a difficult time remaining quiet in the face of opposition. Embracing silence during such times is like trying to stop an active fire hose with your index finger.

Broken men and women, by contrast, can function under incredible pressure. And they are unoffendable.

Brokenness is critical to effective ministry and spiritual power. And God uses the instrument of suffering to bring it about.

T. Austin-Sparks rightly said,

It may be passed on to others through preaching, or through teaching, or through living, but if it is His life it will come out of experiences of suffering. A preacher or teacher who has never suffered will never minister Life.[3]

To make this clearer, here are some of the ways you can waste your sufferings:

- You bleed from them in public.
- You fight against the humans who delivered them.
- You gripe, complain, and become offended with God.
- You rationalize, justify yourself, and blame others.
- You allow yourself to become a victim instead of a student.

Remember, Satan is on a leash. So everything that comes into your life—both wonderful and horrible—must first pass through the loving fingers of your Father before it reaches you. And He uses all of them for your good and His glory (see James 1; 1 Peter 1, 4; Romans 8:28-38; 2 Corinthians 4).

Consider the words of Peter:

> Therefore, since Christ suffered in his body, arm yourselves also with the same attitude, because whoever suffers in the body is done with sin.
>
> 1 PETER 4:1

Peter exhorts the Lord's people to "arm" themselves with a mind to suffer. Consequently, in order to endure suffering and see its good fruit, expect it and recognize that God uses our trials to refine and purify us.

According to Paul, the power of Christ's resurrection life flows from the fellowship of His sufferings (Philippians 3:10).

As both a student and practitioner of music and writing, I've discovered that the greatest art comes out of heartbreak and pain. This is true for the believer and unbeliever alike. A. W. Tozer rightly said, "All great Christians have been wounded souls."[4]

David Wilkerson shared a similar observation:

As we consider those whom God used to stir their
generations, we discover that the elements he used to
shape them were torment, pain, sorrow and failure. . . . To
every true man or woman of God there will come a cup of
pain. . . . So, you want to be a man or woman of God? You
want the hand of the Lord on you? I tell you, you are going
to be served a cup of pain. You will lie in a bed of tears.
You'll weep not so much at physical pain but at something
much worse than that. I'm speaking of the pain of being
bruised and rejected by friends. It is the pain of parents when
children trample their hearts and become strangers to them.
It is the pain between a husband and wife when brick walls
are built up between them.[5]

Indeed, suffering is the lot that awaits you, but it holds within it
treasures that cannot be discovered any other way.

These thoughts have proven true in my own life, enough to motivate me to write an entire book about it.[6]

So expect it, understand it, accept it. And drain all of its positive
juices.

Paul said that we possess a glorious treasure in earthen vessels
(2 Corinthians 4:7). If that treasure is to be released to others, however, the vessel must be broken.

Put another way, only when we are broken bread in the Lord's
hands can He use us to feed the multitudes (Matthew 14:19-21).

This is ministry.

LAW 45

Avoid Toxic People

When I was in my twenties, I didn't understand the difference between a toxic person and a needy person. Most of the Lord's people are needy in some way. But a toxic person is a completely different creature.

Toxic people drain your virtue. If you expose yourself to them long enough, they can cause you to lose your anointing for service.

Some of them are what I call "black holes of ministry." You can pour your life into them for months, even years, and when all is said and done, you've managed only to deplete your spiritual power.

Some people are so toxic that they can rope you into quarrels and strife, something that no servant of God ought to engage in.

> The Lord's servant must not be quarrelsome but must be kind to everyone, able to teach, not resentful.
> 2 TIMOTHY 2:24

> It is to one's honor to avoid strife,
>   but every fool is quick to quarrel.
> PROVERBS 20:3

The power and anointing of God will attract needy people.[1]

But it will also attract toxic souls. Take care, then, that you spend enough time with people who are batteries, not black holes.

Toxic people are usually highly insecure individuals. Their massive insecurity serves as the rudder on a ship bent on its own destruction.

Deeply insecure people remain entrenched in their own fallen minds and emotions, which gives birth to all sorts of jealousies.

All told, avoid toxic people. Paul said as much to Titus:

> Warn a divisive person once, and then warn them a second time. After that, have nothing to do with them.
> TITUS 3:10

And again to the Romans:

> I appeal to you, brothers, to watch out for those who cause divisions and create obstacles contrary to the doctrine that you have been taught; avoid them.
> ROMANS 16:17, ESV

If it's impossible to avoid these people altogether (perhaps you have a family member who is toxic), minimize your interactions. Sometimes enlisting a mediator can help with this.

Sowing Seeds of Discord

Tom just began his first pastorate. He believed that anyone with a need deserved his attention. (Because he was the pastor, you know.)

As a result, Tom responded to everyone in his congregation.

Karen began attending Tom's church, and after each service, she'd compliment his preaching.

She soon began calling the church office, telling the secretary that she had a crisis and needed to meet with Tom in person.

Tom took the first call and spent an hour with Karen.

The pattern continued.

Slowly, Karen began sowing seeds of discord. She started gossiping about different members of the church to both Tom and others. She justified her behavior by saying that Tom and the "more mature people" in the church needed to know about these issues, since they were the "shepherds."

Tom quickly grew suspicious of the people Karen slandered and began looking for ways to address them.

After eight months of this routine, Tom had depleted all his energy.

In time, he discovered that Karen had lied to him. He tracked down her history and contacted several of those who knew her in the past. They all testified to the same thing: "Karen is toxic. She spreads division wherever she goes."

Finally, Tom sat down with Karen and gently corrected her behavior.

He never saw her again.

It took more than a year for Tom to recover from the experience. It took many years for those damaged by Karen's gossip to heal.

Point: Avoid toxic people. If they show up at your church and begin spreading their toxicity, do some research on their background.

The New Testament had a wise habit of sending letters of commendation. A particular church would send a letter to another church (or Christian leader) whenever a person switched fellowships.

The letters were designed to alert the new church that the new member had either a good report or a bad one.[2]

This is a supremely wise but lost practice today. The next best thing is to do your homework and discover the difference between needy people and toxic people.

They're *not* the same.

Do Not Bluff

When I say, "Do not bluff," what do I mean?

Let me illustrate rather than offering a definition.

A young minister breathes fire and brimstone on God's people for not praying enough. After two months of intense praying in his own life, during which time he delivers his most condemning sermons on prayer, the young minister's prayer life recedes to where it becomes almost nonexistent.

He was bluffing.

Someone asks a pastor what he thinks about a difficult text in the Bible. The pastor finds himself incapable of saying three simple words: "I don't know."

So he begins to engage in SMI (share my ignorance).

The minister doesn't know what he's talking about, having never thought about the text. Yet he feels compelled to give an answer.

He therefore reaches into his bag of stock answers and offers a canned response. Why? Because he's the minister, the expert (right?). So he's supposed to know.

He was bluffing.

A young preacher who has only been married for two years sits in his office with an older couple from his congregation who have been married for thirty-five years. The couple is having severe marital problems.

The young preacher offers the couple his best advice on sex, male-female communication, marital struggles, conflict resolution, and intimacy.

He is bluffing. (Do I really have to explain why?)

I trust you get the picture.

As a minister of God's Word, times will come when you'll get pelted with questions that would strike Solomon deaf and dumb.

Never bluff.

I Don't Know

Learn the fine art of saying, "I don't know," three words that break the jaw of many Christian leaders. Then follow it up with, "But I can tell you who can help you with this . . ." or even, "Give me a few weeks to explore your question, and I'll get back to you with my thoughts . . ."

Remember, Paul said, "We know in part" (1 Corinthians 13:9, KJV).

A warped idea floating in the ether of the evangelical world says that if you teach the Scriptures, you must hold a conviction on every issue the Bible mentions.

I don't know who invented this idea, but it's just plain wrong and leads to all sorts of problems.

On the one hand, certainty is overrated. On the other hand, the idea that we can't be certain about anything doesn't square with the New Testament (nor with reality).

Paul said, "We know *in part*" (certainty cannot be attained in everything), but he didn't say, "We know *nothing*" (certainty can be attained for some things).

If you are a believer, especially someone who preaches and teaches, you don't have to know the answer to every question brought to you. It would scare me if you did. It should also scare you (because it's called "delusion").

Taking a position and pontificating on something when you've not done the necessary homework to come to a thoughtful conclusion, or before you've received insight from the Holy Spirit, is just plain reckless. And bluffing (which young men tend to do) is never wise.

So don't buy into the lie. Just because you are in ministry doesn't mean that you have to know all things under the sun or form a conclusion on every topic under heaven (or about every page between the black leather covers).

Forgive the personal example, but my ministry is laser focused on a few themes. And I've immersed myself in those themes my whole adult life. God has so ordered my circumstances and experiences to bring me into a deeper apprehension of those themes. I'm still learning, of course, but I can speak with confidence on those topics.

Countless subjects fall outside of those themes. And other people have far more knowledge in them than I do. When someone asks me about a subject outside my expertise, I typically reply by saying, "I used to know the answer to that question," and then I defer to those who have studied it.

When people look to you for answers in areas that extend beyond your calling, gifting, knowledge, experience, or study, refer them to others whenever you can.

You don't have to have an opinion on every issue that people ask about, and it's profoundly wrong of them to expect you to.

And *nevah evah* be afraid to say, "I don't know."

Saying, "I don't know" is not only honest, but I suspect that the angels in heaven will rejoice (and perhaps fall over) when they hear you utter those words.

Once again, we're back to that thorny issue of humility, a necessary ingredient for possessing God's power.

> Humble yourselves in the sight of the Lord, and He will lift you up.
> JAMES 4:10, NKJV

Put a Handle on It

Elsewhere, I made the statement that most sermons today are swimming lessons on dry land. They are like airplanes that fly high but never land.

The point of both metaphors is that most sermons (and spoken messages) provide no practical exercises for people to implement in their lives.

Imagine a big, beautiful door. Behind the door lie glorious treasures, all of them yours to enjoy.

You get excited.

But there's a problem. The door has no handle, which means you can't open it.

The same thing happens when you preach and teach about knowing the Lord, experiencing His presence, encountering God through Scripture, hearing the Lord's voice, leading others to Christ, praying effectively, making disciples, being transformed, etc., without explaining *how* to practically experience these things.

Unless you find a way to bring God's people into the practical experience of your message, it may be better that you don't speak on it at all. At least, not until you can make it practical.

Your task is to give God's people a way to open the door and tap into the treasures. In other words, put a handle on it.

Ephesians in 3D

Years ago, I took a group of Christians on a guided tour through the book of Ephesians, Paul's most sublime letter.

Before we began, I clearly stated my goal: "We aren't just going to learn Ephesians. Our goal is to experience it. Our mission is to practically handle the riches of Christ contained in this letter."

It took us a full year to get through the letter. The first six months, we lived in Ephesians 1, seeking to drain out of it as many spiritual blessings of Christ as possible.

After every message I delivered, I gave the believers a handle, a practical exercise and action step that everyone could implement to make the letter a living reality.

Some of the exercises were designed to be done individually, while others were for groups of two, three, or four. I participated as well.

What came out of that year astounded me.

People wrote new songs based on the letter. Poems. Skits. Rich fellowship erupted with the Lord Jesus and with one another. Scores of glorious meetings took place in which everyone in the fellowship shared the riches of Christ.

I look back at that year as a spiritual cloudburst for all of us, an unforgettable time with the Lord Jesus and His body. It was beautiful. We lived two or three blocks from heaven that year.

When it ended, we hadn't just learned Ephesians; we'd discovered the Christ of Ephesians. We not only went through the letter; the letter went through us.

Therefore, whenever you preach or teach, put a handle on it.

Make what you teach or preach so practical that God's people can experience it. This will move what you say out of the notebook and into the heart. And it's yet another path to spiritual power.

LAW 48

Realize It Doesn't Work

This law is difficult to communicate without being misunderstood. But I'll do my best.

If you're in your twenties or early thirties, you may not have lived long enough to relate to what I'm about to say. If so, reread this chapter fifteen years from now.

Here's the essence of this law:

The Christian life as the New Testament envisions it does not work.

The church as the New Testament conceives it doesn't work.

Relationships as the New Testament teaches them do not work.

Read the book of Acts and the epistles and see if you can find a perfect Christian, a perfect church, a perfect co-working relationship, a perfect marriage, perfect children, perfect parents, etc.

If you read carefully—and honestly—you'll find failure, breakdown, damage, tragedy, and a whole lot of first-class messes.

Everything in the spiritual life breaks down. *All* of it tends toward entropy. The *whole thing* follows the second law of thermodynamics.

The bulk of the New Testament was written to churches that were in high-voltage crises.

Yet in the middle of the chaos, you will also discover something else, something beautiful: God's presence and power.

Both are peppered throughout the messes.

In the New Testament, we have a wedding of glory and gore, failure and triumph, breakdown and repair. The two are ongoing, dwelling in each other's presence.

Does It Work?

Years ago, someone who heard me speak about body life in a conference asked me, "Frank, does it work? Can we have Christ-centered community like the churches in the first century and what you've written about in your early books?"[1]

"Yes, absolutely," I answered. "It works. But it works about as well as it did in the first century!"

Let me break that statement apart.

In one sense, it doesn't work at all. Again, read Acts and all the epistles with an eye to answering the question, "Does Christian community really work?"

You'll have to answer, "No, not really."

Yet in another sense, it works wonderfully—*for what God designed it for*.

If the standard is perfection, it doesn't work.

But if the end game is the transformation of those who mean business with God, then slowly but surely, it works.

Some Christians will be transformed in the midst of the mess. Others will reject the inward transformational work of the cross, pack their bags, and go on their merry way, either back into the world or to a more comfortable individualistic "Christian" existence.[2]

My point is simple. The Christian life doesn't "work." And neither does the church as God intended. And neither do relationships.

But God is after something *much* deeper than what "works."

And the quicker you learn that lesson, the greater your service to God will be. The Lord is always "working" in the midst of failure, chaos, and breakdown.

But Jesus replied, "My Father is always working, and so am I."
JOHN 5:17, NLT

Straight Talk to Leaders

With forethought and deliberation, I have kept this book fairly short. But there's more to be said.

Much more.

That being translated means: If you plan to write me a flaming email, scolding me for not addressing *xyz* in the book (not very "Christian" of you, by the way), stand down. The story isn't over.

Consequently, the web page below contains talks I've given to leaders that have never been publicly released.

These talks expand some of the themes presented in this book as well as introducing new, related topics.

They also provide many practical handles that you can apply to your own life and ministry.

In addition, I've added six more codas on the same web page:

- Coda VI: Toss Out Your Notes

- Coda VII: Practice Radical Generosity

- Coda VIII: Discouraged by Better Preachers

- Coda IX: Stealing, Borrowing, and Inspiring

- Coda X: Three Laws of the Harvest

- Coda XI: Five Must-Read Books

Just go to 48Laws.net to access the talks and the extra codas.

I now urge you to read the following codas in this book.

When you finish them, I think you'll understand why.

I also encourage you to read chapter 84 ("A Special Word to Christian Workers") in my book *Hang On, Let Go*.

A Final Point

Sometimes pastors, preachers, teachers, missionaries, and church planters ask me for personal mentoring.

For this reason, we've put together The Insurgence Experience, a one-year mentoring program for people in ministry done over Zoom. It also includes one in-person gathering.

You can peruse all the details and fill out the application at TheInsurgence.org/ixp.

The Danger of God's Power

There is a dark side of ministry that is rarely discussed. And if you're not careful, you could succumb to it.

When God gives His power to someone, it exposes them. It humbles one person and destroys another.

Consider two recent converts. Both are young men who seek to be "endued" with God's power.

The Lord graciously grants both their requests.

The first man begins using God's power for his own ends. His original prayer was fueled by the desire to draw large crowds, zap demons, and do great wonders.

He shares space with the uber-ambitious Simon, who offered to pay Peter good money to harness God's power (Acts 8:9-24).

The second man wants to magnify his Lord and advance God's kingdom. He realizes he can't accomplish either without being endued with God's power. So he prays accordingly.

When God's Power Becomes Unsafe

There is a sober stewardship attached to the power of God.

Miraculous power operates by gift, not character.

A Christian walking in the flesh, therefore, can still operate in the miraculous gifts of the Holy Spirit.

A carnal believer can speak in tongues, perform healings, and even receive spiritual insight. If you don't believe me, just read 1 Corinthians 14.

The Corinthian believers lived in massive carnality (chapters 1 to 12), yet they continued to operate abundantly in spiritual gifts.

Paul makes it clear that a person can speak in tongues and even receive spiritual understanding and prophetic utterance yet lack love—the supreme mark of spiritual character:

> If I speak in the tongues of men or of angels, but do not have love, I am only a resounding gong or a clanging cymbal. If I have the gift of prophecy and can fathom all mysteries and all knowledge, and if I have a faith that can move mountains, but do not have love, I am nothing.
>
> 1 CORINTHIANS 13:1-2

I grew up in a movement in which many Christians got drunk on God's power. They chased power more than they chased Jesus. They were so obsessed with the miraculous that they lost sight of Christ.

Even worse, some in the leadership were power hungry, trying to harness God's power to meet their own ends.

I could singe your ears with stories of men who had impressive displays of miraculous power but who engaged in all sorts of perversions and drug/alcohol abuse behind closed doors.

These men lived on the edge of hell as they preached victory and performed signs and wonders.

As a student of history, I marvel at the stories of the great American evangelists during the post–World War II era. Many of them were the most powerfully gifted men of their time, but they destroyed their ministries by making foolish decisions. (Billy Graham was a rare exception.)

Samson, King Saul, and Balaam are not alone in the long trail of souls who operated in powerful, miraculous gifts, but who woefully lacked character.

Saul could prophesy by the Spirit of God while at the same time holding murder in his heart—and even acting on it (see 1 Samuel 19).

Though God gives His gifts by grace, and as a general rule they cannot be revoked (Romans 11:29), in some cases the Lord removes His anointing from a servant because of persistent disobedience.

This is a tragic state known as an "Ichabod" situation.[1] The flow stops, the brook dries up, the anointing lifts, the well quits giving water, and the power evaporates. The glory departs.

Here's a word of warning: If you try to harness God's power for your own aims, you're dealing with the wrong God. In the words of C. S. Lewis, Jesus Christ is not a tame lion.[2] He will not be harnessed nor controlled.

Where Power Is Safe

God never gives His power to you or me to wield as individuals. He gives His power to the bride of Christ, the ekklesia.

Whenever I see men wielding God's power as isolated individuals, I immediately see imminent destruction. The power of God on an individual will destroy him. It's safe only when that person remains properly connected to other members of the body.

In every case I can think of when an individual abused God's power, that person was disconnected from the body of Christ. Yes, they may have attended church services. In fact, they may have even regularly preached in them.

But that's not the same as having a living experience of the body of Christ, where close-knit relationships are forged and members temper one another.

I'm also impressed that Jesus didn't try to gain fame through His signs and wonders. Have you ever noticed that the Lord never made a production out of healing the sick? When Jesus performed a healing, He virtually always told that person not to tell anyone.[3] We see a certain modesty in Christ whenever He exercised His power.

God's power is available to accomplish His will, but it's so easy to corrupt, pervert, and make cheap and common.

But wait, it gets even worse.

Malignant Narcissism

Spiritual power causes some people, perhaps many, to believe they can handle everything on their own. These befuddled souls are marked by titanic arrogance mixed with paranoia. They are erratic narcissists and serial liars who have an unwarranted confidence in their own sagacity. They are rude, crude, insensitive, judgmental, and as crooked as a dog's hind leg.

They are also prone to violate Proverbs 27:2, regularly lathering themselves up with praise.

In some twisted way, they believe they have a right to such self-indulgence because they carry God's anointing.

The same thing happens when individuals acquire political power. Many of them turn into insufferable human beings. Privilege has a toxic influence on most humans. How ironic that those gifted with God's power slip into the same temptations. Unfortunately, malignant narcissism abounds in both the political and religious worlds.

But a major fall awaits such people. They will move from a powerful place to a place of deep weakness. This is God's generous grace, because power is made perfect in weakness (2 Corinthians 12:9), and only the weak and poor in spirit can heal the broken and needy.

It was said of Jesus that He would not break a bruised reed nor snuff out a smoldering wick (Matthew 12:20). In the ancient world, smoldering wicks signaled that they should be extinguished and replaced with new ones. Bruised reeds couldn't measure accurately, so they too had to be discarded and replaced.

Strikingly, Jesus didn't discard or replace the damaged, the weak, and the broken.

He healed them.

As the One gentle and lowly in heart (Matthew 11:29), our Lord consistently helped the least, the lost, and the lowest.

By contrast, those who take God's power for granted not only discard the broken; they run over them.

With weakness comes the power to heal the weak. Without weakness, God's power becomes a dangerous thing. So be careful.

A Most Dangerous Prayer

Coming back to the beginning of this chapter, one of the most dangerous prayers a Christian can utter is the request for God's power.

Very often, what lies hidden behind such prayers is the unspoken ambition for fame and the desire to be regarded as a "spiritual giant" admired by many.[4]

But before you can be safe to God's people, it's critical that you become aware of the dark intentions lurking in your heart. You must first slay the monster of human ambition.

Personally, I tremble when I hear young people ask God for power.

If the Lord is merciful enough to answer your prayer, I have one word of advice: *Duck!*

The Lord will arrange your circumstances in such a way that you will be leveled to the ground, broken but fit for the Master's use.

God's Spirit will take you through deep waters to accomplish this.

The earth does not need more outwardly powerful people. It needs inwardly transformed people. And only the latter can be trusted with God's power.

If you have an unhealthy appetite for power, you'll experience serious indigestion and worse.

Let us be careful stewards of the holy things of God, broken and humble vessels properly coordinated with other members of the body of Christ.

The power of God in an unbroken vessel is a toxic thing.

Never forget that.

Three Instruments

Every person called to the Lord's work possesses three instruments: a jackhammer, a surgeon's knife, and an anesthetic syringe.

The test of spiritual discernment and wise leadership is to know when to use which instrument.

Some are more gifted at using the jackhammer. This is the deconstructive ministry of the genuinely prophetic. Such people aren't tailors who thread a needle. They are wrecking balls.

Others are more adept at wielding the surgeon's knife, resolving people's spiritual problems with gentleness yet pinpoint accuracy.

Still others are more schooled at administering the pain-relieving balm of anesthesia.

But everyone called to the Lord's work must learn how and when to use each instrument.

One of the things that aids in this endeavor is to become part of a ministry team.

Unfortunately, most leaders today are solo acts with no interest in working with their peers. Their penchant for independence hinders their spiritual usefulness and hampers the kingdom of God from advancing.

Don't make that mistake.

Most of the pastors I have known throughout my life couldn't answer most of the "hard questions" I pelted them with. But I didn't stop there. I looked beyond them.

As for the Old Testament and the reliability of Scripture, I wrestled with all of that, and I found completely satisfying answers. Unfortunately, the answers are largely unknown in the mainstream Christian world, where paying for Facebook ads and YouTube views dominates. Everything else gets lost. It's a bit like US presidential elections. The smartest, brightest, most capable, most gifted leaders in the country can't run because they lack the big bucks. So they remain largely unknown to the world.

He didn't mention this one, but I have money hidden in my socks that says he'd agree. I've always found "the Christian side hug" rather silly.

This former Christian leader deserves a taco. (Forget that. I just wanted to make sure you're still paying attention.) Indeed, if you keep pulling at the threads of a sweater, it will unravel until the sweater disappears. But in the case of Jesus Christ, if this is your experience, you're pulling on the wrong sweater.

The genuine sweater is available if you look hard enough—and it can't be unraveled.

So it was for me and millions of others.

My point is that this leader, and others like him, never went to any of us who could identify with everything he wrote, who have even published books and podcasts offering solutions out of real-life experience.

Thankfully, God is raising up a new generation of hot hearts for Jesus Christ who have the fire of the gospel of the kingdom burning inside them. And I'm honored to know many of you.

When the day comes when this tribe takes to the streets, the fire burning in their bellies won't be for a cause, no matter how good that cause may be.

It will be for Jesus Christ and His everlasting kingdom.

The Insurgence has begun . . . don't miss it!

The bottom line: Unless you have genuinely encountered the Lord Jesus Christ, you'll always be in danger of falling away from "the faith."

But if Jesus Christ gets into your pores, it's impossible to scrub Him out.

CODA IV

Passing the Torch

We commonly use the phrase "passing the torch" to depict the act of passing on a charge or responsibility to another person. The metaphor comes from the ancient Greek torch races, where one runner passed a lighted torch to another runner who carried the torch farther.

I've given a lot of thought to the idea of passing the torch in the Lord's work. Each decade, a number of God's choicest servants pass on. But few of them ever pass the torch on to a younger soul.

This is a great tragedy. And it's one of the reasons why the Lord's highest work has only moved in millimeters (instead of miles).

Several years ago, I was having lunch with a friend who told me about a dream Myles Munroe had before he passed away. Myles saw an Olympic runner lying in a coffin with his hands clutched to a baton. His fists were holding the baton so tightly that it was no small task to pry it from his hands.

The point of the dream was that many of the Lord's servants refuse to pass the torch to the younger generation.

When my friend told me this story, he wasn't aware that this subject had been on my mind all year.

Many of the Lord's choicest vessels will pass on in the coming years. The question is: Will they pass the torch to another servant of God, or will they die with it in their hands?

Let me make two observations about this question:

Observation 1: Whenever a servant of God refuses to pass on the torch, it is usually for one of three reasons.

- *Arrogance.* The servant thinks too highly of himself. His inflated view blinds him from recognizing and honoring the Lord's calling, gifting, and operation in others, especially the person to whom God has called him to hand the torch. In his eyes, no one is "worthy" enough (which reveals a stunning lack of self-awareness).

- *Jealousy.* The servant doesn't want to share the glory with anyone else. When others demonstrate signs of God's anointing and favor, instead of cheering them on, these leaders turn green.

- *Ignorance.* The idea of passing on the knowledge, experience, and charge of their ministries to someone younger never crosses their minds. So it all dies with the older servant of God.

By contrast, servants of God who have leveled their egos at the cross—including the jealousy and arrogance that goes with it—are eager to pass the torch on.

Observation 2: A servant of God who is unwilling to pass the torch will often have it taken away because the person whom God destined to carry it will end up seizing it.

Though God's highest and best is for the older to willingly pass the torch on to the younger, the call of God sometimes compels the younger to grasp the torch nonetheless. Even though this isn't the ideal (and it involves its own drawbacks), it's far better for the advance of the kingdom than allowing the torch to be buried in the grave.

I, therefore, wish to issue an indelible challenge to every servant of God, both young and old (for the former will become the latter one day).

If God has handed you a torch to bear during your lifetime, make the decision *now* that you will not allow arrogance, jealousy, or ignorance to keep you from passing it on to someone else. If you die with it in your hands, it only reveals one thing: You never understood that it wasn't yours to begin with.

And to all younger servants of God: Find an older laborer in the Lord's vineyard whom you respect, who has a unique contribution and God's favor on his or her life, and intentionally reach out to that person directly, so when the time comes for the leader to pass on the torch, you will be on their radar.

The world is dying to find men and women who are burning. Firebrands who can rain glory down from heaven and preach like a house on fire. Those who can rip loose with their message of Christ and help God's people to soar high.

But such rare souls must find older, more seasoned, more experienced mentors. Otherwise, they will eventually flame out, sometimes in ways they'll regret for the rest of their lives.

A Nicodemus Moment

Years ago, I received an invitation to speak to a group of pastors, teachers, and leaders for a two-day retreat.

On the last day, they asked me to share some snapshots of Christ-centered community from my own experience.

I told the story of one such community, a body of believers that discovered Jesus Christ in the depths and learned to love one another through thick or thin.

They also learned how to have New Testament–styled church meetings where every member functioned, sharing the riches of Christ through their various gifts—all without a facilitator present.

Their gatherings and their community life were under the headship of Jesus Christ.

One of my closing comments was that this group of believers had discovered that Christ was alive enough to be the head of His own church, not in rhetoric but in reality.

They certainly had their share of problems and issues, as did every church in the first century. But they also discovered how to find the Lord in their midst.

The examples I gave of the work of the Holy Spirit in this group were stunning. And they made a tremendous impact on my own life and ministry, all these years later.

When I finished, I observed two reactions in the room.

One was amazement. Some leaders had never seen or heard

anything like what I described. Later, they quizzed me privately. Those people greatly impressed me.

Their hunger for the Lord displayed itself in their insightful comments and discerning questions.

The other group didn't quite understand what I was talking about. They had no context for it, so they politely listened and then went on to other things, never asking a single question.

One gentleman in the room was both a professor and a pastor. After hearing me rehearse story after story about the amazing things that happened and can still happen when a group of Christians discovers together how to live by the indwelling life of Christ, he declared his opinion with the group.

"What you've just described," he said, "is a sociological reality called group form dynamics."

This man had just heard the living testimony of Jesus Christ through His body, and he responded with, "You're describing a sociological reality."

Here was a leader in the Christian world, a pastor in a very large denomination and a professor, and that's all he heard.

I felt as though I was interacting with an atheist.

"I believe that Jesus Christ exists and that He's real," I said. "I also believe that He lives in His people, and when they learn to live by His life, they can express Him in remarkable ways, shaming principalities and powers in other realms. That's what this group of simple Christians discovered."

The conversation then moved on to other things.

I tell this story, all these years later, to highlight a Nicodemus moment.

Consider what Jesus said to Nicodemus:

"You are Israel's teacher," said Jesus, "and do you not understand these things? Very truly I tell you, we speak of what we know, and we testify to what we have seen, but still you people do not accept our testimony. I have spoken to

you of earthly things and you do not believe; how then will
you believe if I speak of heavenly things?"

JOHN 3:10-12

Just because someone may sport a clerical collar, pastor a church,
answer to "reverend," or hold more degrees than a thermometer, it
does not indicate that they know the Lord very well.

Don't mishear me. I have close friends who are pastors and professors who have a deep and authentic walk with Jesus Christ. They also
can perceive when He's working.

However, just because someone is part of the clergy or they matric-
ulated from seminary, it doesn't ensure that they are spiritual or can
discern spiritual things.

The sad fact is we have many Nicodemuses around today.

They may hold PhDs in theology or ministry, but that doesn't
mean they know Christ well or are living by His indwelling life. Our
situation is no different today than it was in ancient Israel when God
became enfleshed and broke into human history.

T. Austin-Sparks put his finger on the problem this way:

What is the nature of your relationship with Christ? You
may believe in the Christian doctrine of the Deity of Christ,
and believe in it very intensely. But if it is only doctrine, a
tenet of the Creed, an objective fact concerning Christ, it
will not carry you through the terrific experiences which lie
in the path of true Christians. John said that the object of
his writing his Gospel was that we might believe that Jesus
is the Son of God, and that believing we might have life in
His name. But he took pains to show that those who did so
believe, had an experimental basis for their faith. How and
why do you believe? Can you say truly—"because something
has happened in me for which there is no accounting apart
from God Himself. Emotions, reasonings, persuasions,
cannot account for it. Human personalities, psychology,

or any human or natural factor cannot account for it. It required God Almighty, and I found Him in Jesus Christ. It was the voice of the Son of God, and I lived, and live."[1]

May the tribe of the unknown yet insightful Annas and Simeons (Luke 2:25-38) increase, for they had eyes to see in a religious culture that was blind.

Bottom line. Never be impressed with mere externals when it comes to spiritual knowledge and experience.

Remember that Jesus of Nazareth was a day laborer. He had no formal religious training, unlike the scribes and priests of His day (who were spiritually blind).

Neither did the twelve men whom He chose to carry on His work.

Formal religious training isn't bad. It can be helpful. But it's no guarantee in equipping women and men to know their Lord well and follow their spiritual instincts.

NOTES

PRELUDE: EFFECTIVE MINISTRY AND SPIRITUAL POWER

1. If you minister outside the institutional church, I recommend that you supplement this book with one of my earlier books, *Finding Organic Church* (Colorado Springs: David C. Cook, 2009), which deals with the apostolic ministry of planting authentic kingdom communities.
2. Matthew 3:16; Isaiah 42:1. Jesus quotes the passage and applies it to Himself in Luke 4:16-21.
3. In Acts 1:1, Luke says that he previously wrote about what Jesus *began* to do and teach (referring to the book of Luke). The book of Acts, then, is a record of the *continuation* of what Jesus did and taught through His body.
4. T. Austin-Sparks, *Power with God*, booklet reprinted from *A Witness and a Testimony* magazine, January–October 1967, vol. 45, no.1—45, no. 5.
5. The mastermind was called "MinistryMind." It's since changed to a mentoring program. For details, see MinistryMind.org.
6. See "Judge vs. Judge Not—Which Is It?" at frankviola.org/judging.

LAW 1: NEVER HURT GOD'S PEOPLE

1. "You have not so learned Christ" is Paul's language, beautifully put in Ephesians 4:20, NKJV.
2. I make a case for this interpretation in "Rethinking Paul's Thorn in the Flesh" at frankviola.org/paulsthornintheflesh.

LAW 2: DO NOT BE A PEOPLE PLEASER

1. I heard Tozer give this definition in a spoken message he delivered long ago.
2. I talk about these core values—which are nonnegotiable—in chapter 39 of *Hang On, Let Go* (Carol Stream, IL: Tyndale, 2021).

LAW 3: BEWARE THE EMPTY HOUSE

1. In the Beautiful Pursuit Master Class, I share in detail how to fill your house by pursuing the Lord in various and sundry ways. You can check out the class at frankviola.org/classes.

LAW 4: IT TAKES ONE TO MAKE ONE

1. The Galatians in 3D Master Class has set many ministers and non-leaders free from condemnation, guilt, shame, religious obligation, and duty. You can check out free samples at frankviola.org/classes.
2. Watchman Nee, *The Release of the Spirit* (Indianapolis: Sure Foundation, 1965), 9.

LAW 5: DETEST CELEBRITISM

1. I discuss the biblical principle of Babylon in chapter 17 of *From Eternity to Here* (Colorado Springs: David C. Cook, 2009).
2. You can see mine at frankviola.org/faq.
3. See Mark 5:35 and Luke 8:49.
4. François Fénelon, *Let Go* (n.p., GodSounds, 2017), 9.
5. T. Austin-Sparks, *Leadership and Ministry* (Tulsa, OK: Emmanuel Church, 2015), 7–8.

LAW 6: AVOID BURNOUT

1. I credit my friend Leonard Sweet with this phrase.
2. From a spoken message by T. Austin-Sparks entitled "Christ Our All," delivered in Gümligen, Switzerland, in 1935.
3. Though this cannot be proven, one gets this impression when Paul speaks about Epaphroditus in Philippians 2.
4. Bonnie Stiernberg, "'Is It Better to Burn Out Than to Fade Away' and Other Impossible Questions," *Paste*, July 1, 2016.

LAW 7: LEAVE THE RESULTS WITH GOD

1. For instance, some pastors are actually called to the apostolic work. Others are gifted at administration, but they aren't called to preach or teach.
2. I discuss how to practically hear the Lord's voice in the second half of Leonard Sweet and Frank Viola, *Jesus Speaks: Learning to Recognize & Respond to the Lord's Voice* (Nashville: Thomas Nelson, 2016).
3. See Frank Viola, "God's View of a Woman," *Beyond Evangelical* (blog), frankviola.org/godsview.
4. The Gospels rarely inform us that Jesus loved a particular individual. Lazarus, Mary and Martha, and the writer of the Gospel of John are some of the exceptions. While Jesus was and is love incarnate, it's significant when the Scripture tells us that He loved a specific person.
5. Examples: Matthew 13:15; Mark 3:5; Acts 16:14; 2 Corinthians 6:11, 13. For a list of significant biblical texts on the state of a person's heart when they hear preaching or teaching, see Frank Viola, "Dull of Hearing," *Beyond Evangelical* (blog), frankviola.org/dullofhearing.

LAW 8: OVERCOME DISCOURAGEMENT

1. Frank Viola, *Hang On, Let Go* (Carol Stream, IL: Tyndale House, 2021), 213.

2. Based on the latest data I've seen, more than two thousand pastors leave the pastoral role in the USA each month. For many of them, a crisis of conscience leads them out of that role, and they begin serving God in other ways. Some have disputed this figure (for obvious reasons), but even if one-fourth of that is the true number, it's still a staggering number.

LAW 9: FIND SPIRITUAL SATISFACTION

1. Exodus 32.
2. Dallas Willard, "The Secret to Ministry Satisfaction," ChurchLeaders.com, August 12, 2018.
3. Willard, "The Secret to Ministry Satisfaction."
4. Blaise Pascal, *Pensées*, 139.
5. Willard, "The Secret to Ministry Satisfaction."
6. For some examples, listen to episode #55 of the *Insurgence* podcast, "How an Insurgent Approaches Scripture" and read the article "Aware of His Presence," at insurgencebook.com/Aware.pdf.
7. T. Austin-Sparks, "On Knowing the Lord," *A Witness and a Testimony* magazine, Nov-Dec 1930, vol. 8–6.

LAW 10: REFUSE TO TAKE OFFENSE

1. I explain this in episode #49 of the *Christ Is All* podcast, "Beyond Evangelical."
2. Matthew 11:6, ESV.

LAW 11: LOWER YOUR EXPECTATIONS

1. A. W. Tozer, *And He Dwelt Among Us: Teachings from the Gospel of John* (Ventura, CA: Regal, 2009), 135.
2. See Romans 15:14; 2 Corinthians 2:3; 7:6; 8:22; Galatians 5:10; 2 Thessalonians 3:4; Philemon 1:21; Hebrews 6:9.

LAW 12: USE HUMOR TO CONNECT AND DISARM

1. Leonard Sweet and Frank Viola, *Jesus: A Theography* (Nashville: Thomas Nelson, 2012), 200–202.
2. Rick and Kay Warren interview, *Religion & Ethics Newsweekly*, September 1, 2006.
3. G. K. Chesterton, *Orthodoxy* (San Francisco: Ignatius Press, 1995), 127–128.
4. To the pedantic, punctilious, and oversensitive, I am aware that, ultimately, we follow Jesus. But Paul said, "Become followers of me, as I also [am] of Christ" (1 Corinthians 11:1, LSV). He also commended a church for imitating him (1 Thessalonians 1:6). See also his words to Timothy in 2 Timothy 3:10-11. Therefore, I'm using the phrase "follow a man" the same way Paul did.

LAW 13: BE A RESERVOIR, NOT A CANAL

1. Bernard of Clairvaux, *Song of Songs*, Sermon 18.
2. Bernard, *Song of Songs*.

3. *The Complete Works of C. H. Spurgeon*, volume 59: Sermons 3335–3386 (Harrington, DE: Delmarva Publications, 2013).
4. Andrew Murray, *The Deeper Christian Life* (New York: Cosimo Classics, 2007), 87.
5. A. W. Tozer, *Born After Midnight* (Camp Hill, PA: WingSpread, 2008), 152.
6. James L. Snyder, *The Life of A. W. Tozer: In Pursuit of God* (Camp Hill, PA: Christian Publications, 1991), 10.

LAW 14: RECEIVE CORRECTION
1. Frank Viola, *Revise Us Again* (Colorado Springs: David C. Cook, 2011), 115.
2. I discuss the difference between being a victim and a student in episode #140 of the *Christ Is All* podcast, "Help When Your World is Crumbling."

LAW 15: DISTINGUISH BETWEEN CRITICS
1. Frank Viola, "Three Kinds of Critics & How to Respond to Them," *Beyond Evangelical* (blog), frankviola.org/2013/02/13/threekindsofcritics.
2. Martin Luther King, Jr., "Letter from Birmingham Jail," April 16, 1963.
3. The exception to this is if you are specifically called to expose a troll. Some people are called to that task, but in doing so, they are not engaging the troll directly. They are instead exposing the troll's track record, history of dishonesty, and any legal or ethical violations—such as defamation violations, social media suspensions, and church excommunications. Christians who expose the sins of others, however, should always first go alone and privately to the person who is trolling. And then, if necessary, privately with witnesses, following the steps set forth in Matthew 18, asking the individual to repent before their transgression is exposed publicly.
4. Quoted in Charles Morris, *Battling for the Right: The Life Story of Theodore Roosevelt* (n.p., 1910), 354–355.

LAW 16: EXPECT MISUNDERSTANDINGS
1. Episode #42 of the *Christ Is All* podcast, "A City Whose Builder and Maker Is God." The question and answer section wasn't retained.
2. The author's paraphrase.
3. The exception is if you're telling a parable or story in order to deliberately sift your hearers, as Jesus did in Mark 4:9-12. But that's an entirely different subject, one that's beyond the scope of this book.

LAW 17: GUARD AGAINST SELF-RIGHTEOUSNESS
1. Leonard Sweet and Frank Viola, *Jesus: A Theography* (Nashville: Thomas Nelson, 2012), 208.
2. I discuss this theme in detail in my book *From Eternity to Here: Rediscovering the Ageless Purpose of God* (Colorado Springs: David C. Cook, 2009).
3. See frankviola.org/onesideofstory.
4. Kahlil Gibran, *The Kahlil Gibran Reader: Inspirational Writings* (New York: Citadel Press, 2006), 39.

5. Philip Yancey, "Homosexuality," philipyancey.com (blog), July 8, 2010.
6. This section previously published in Frank Viola, "How (Not) to Correct Another Christian," ChurchLeaders.com, June 18, 2012.
7. Watchman Nee, *The Joyful Heart* (Fort Washington, PA: CLC Publications, 1970), 230.
8. You can listen to the follow-up to this chapter, episode #108 on the *Christ Is All* podcast, "How Not to Receive Correction."

LAW 18: AVOID ISOLATION
1. For details, listen to episode #41 of the *Insurgence* podcast, "Keeping Unstained by the World."
2. I recommend that you listen to episode #99 of the *Christ Is All* podcast, "7 Ways to Destroy a Friendship."

LAW 19: DEVELOP AN INSTINCT FOR THE CROSS
1. In my book *Hang On, Let Go*, I discuss a number of other dimensions of the cross of Christ using Scripture, specifically the trials and sufferings that God allows to come into our lives.
2. 1 Samuel 19:23.
3. 1 Samuel 22:17.

LAW 21: EMPLOY FASTING WITH PRAYER
1. I realize that the consensus among contemporary scholars is that Mark 16 isn't authentic. That may be true, but we cannot be absolutely certain since we don't possess the original New Testament manuscripts. The chapter has been quoted since the second century by a number of church fathers, and what's found in it is confirmed by other parts of the New Testament. So I have no problem quoting from it.
2. Fasting is also a means of mourning. See Matthew 9:15 and James 4:8-10 (though the latter text doesn't specifically mention fasting, it fits the spirit of it).
3. I explain this in my article "How to Break an Addiction," frankviola.org /addictions.
4. For further insights into the practice of fasting, check out episode #39 of the *Insurgence* podcast, "Fasting and the Kingdom of God."

LAW 23: RESIST BITTERNESS
1. Frank Viola, *God's Favorite Place on Earth* (Colorado Springs: David C. Cook, 2013), 35.
2. For details, see chapter 71 in Frank Viola, *Hang On, Let Go* (Tyndale Momentum, 2021).
3. Viola, *God's Favorite Place on Earth*, 190.

LAW 24: SERVE IN THE SPIRIT
1. Yes, that's a joke. See Frank Viola, *From Eternity to Here* (Colorado Springs: David C. Cook, 2009).

2. T. Austin-Sparks, *An Explanation of the Nature and History of "This Ministry"* (Tulsa, OK: Emmanuel Church, 2004), 7–8.

LAW 25: DEFY THE CONVENTIONAL WISDOM

1. For details, see Frank Viola and George Barna, *Pagan Christianity?* (Carol Stream, IL: Tyndale, 2008), chapter 3.
2. The New Testament is clear that Jesus, the Word made flesh, created all things in the visible universe: John 1:3; Colossians 1:15-16; Hebrews 1:1-2.
3. Adapted from Frank Viola, "3 Lessons Every Writer, Speaker, Blogger, and Musician Can Learn from Led Zeppelin," ChurchLeaders.com, March 5, 2012. Benjamin Franklin quote is from Robert Walsh, "Life of Benjamin Franklin," *Delaplaine's Repository of the Lives and Portraits of Distinguished Americans* (Philadelphia, 1815–1817), II, 52.

LAW 26: KEEP YOUR HANDS CLEAN

1. Frank Laubach, *You Are My Friends* (New York: Harper & Brothers, 1942), 34.
2. Upton Sinclair, *I, Candidate for Governor: And How I Got Licked* (Berkeley: University of California Press, 1934, 1994), 109.
3. From a spoken message called "A Holy Nation" delivered by T. Austin-Sparks in 1960.

LAW 27: UNVEIL CHRIST

1. Frank Viola, *From Eternity to Here: Rediscovering the Ageless Purpose of God* (Colorado Springs: David C. Cook, 2009), 299–300.
2. I discuss these two enemies of the gospel in detail in *Insurgence: Reclaiming the Gospel of the Kingdom* (Grand Rapids: Baker, 2018).
3. See Insurgence.org for details.
4. Albert Edward Thompson, *The Life of A. B. Simpson* (New York: The Christian Alliance Publishing Company, 1920), 196.
5. *Jesus: A Theography* unveils Christ from Genesis to Revelation and explains the Christocentric hermeneutic that Jesus gave His disciples.
6. I give credit to Oswald J. Smith for this insight.
7. I speak more about this in episode #76 of the *Insurgence* podcast in my conversation with a seminary professor at Asbury. The episode is called "Kingdom Ministry: Past, Present, Future." Among other things, I talk about unveiling Jesus Christ through one's preaching.
8. QuoteInvestigator.com suggests that contemporary versions of this quote may have been adapted from Antoine de Saint-Exupéry, *Citadelle*, LXXV (Paris: Gallimard, 1948), 687, but definitive attribution cannot be found.
9. The "how" deserves another book, but I go into it in The Insurgence Experience, which is designed for those who regularly preach and teach. See TheInsurgence.org/ixp.

LAW 28: MANAGE CONFLICT

1. If this is news to you, I invite you to carefully read 2 Corinthians 1, 6, 11, and 12 as well as 1 Corinthians 4.

2. Zechariah 13:6.
3. T. Austin-Sparks, *Daily Open Windows* (Tulsa, OK: Emmanuel Church, 2012), 241.
4. David Wilkerson, "The Making of a Man of God," WorldChallenge.org (blog).
5. Mark 5:13.
6. Matthew 8:28-34.

LAW 29: DO NOT COMPROMISE
1. Frank C. Laubach, *You Are My Friends* (Harper and Brothers, 1942), 126.
2. Watchman Nee, *The Joyful Heart* (Fort Washington, PA: CLC Publications, 1977), 175.

LAW 30: EQUIP AND EMPOWER, DO NOT CONTROL
1. Leonard Sweet and Frank Viola, *Jesus Manifesto* (Nashville: Thomas Nelson, 2010), 25–26.
2. Preaching on the reality of eternal judgment to the lost is another story. "Knowing therefore the terror of the Lord, we persuade men" (2 Corinthians 5:11, KJV). "As he [Paul] reasoned with them about righteousness and self-control and the coming day of judgment, Felix became frightened" (Acts 24:25, NLT). "And others save with fear, pulling them out of the fire; hating even the garment spotted by the flesh" (Jude 23, KJV).
3. Many leaders have found my Spiritual Graffiti: Galatians in 3D Master Class of help in this area. See frankviola.org/galatians.

LAW 31: REMOVE THE RELIGIOUS MASK
1. Matthew 6:5-8.
2. Frank Viola and George Barna, *Pagan Christianity?* (Carol Stream, IL: Tyndale House Publishers, 2008), chapter 5.
3. This metaphor comes from 1 Samuel 17:38-40. The lesson is don't try to be someone you're not.
4. Rudyard Kipling, "If." Public domain.

LAW 32: STAY IN SCHOOL
1. In chapter 10 of *Pagan Christianity?* ("Christian Education"), I discuss the origin of our Bible colleges and seminaries and the general fruit they produce.
2. T. Austin-Sparks and some (not all) of Watchman Nee's work is amazing. You can see the books I recommend by both Austin-Sparks and Nee on my 100 best Christian books ever written list at frankviola.org/top100.
3. See chapter 10 of *Pagan Christianity?* ("Christian Education").
4. Dallas Willard, "The Secret to Ministry Satisfaction," ChurchLeaders.com, August 12, 2018.
5. Fred Shapiro, *The New Yale Book of Quotations* (New Haven, CT: Yale University Press, 2021), 259.
6. You can see the list at frankviola.org/top100.

LAW 33: EMBRACE CO-WORKING

1. In *Finding Organic Church*, I compare how Jesus trained the Twelve in Galilee with how Paul trained workers in Ephesus.
2. See my article "My Vision for a Ministry Dream Team" at InsurgenceBook .com/DreamTeam.pdf.

LAW 34: BE A CHANNEL, NOT A POND

1. Frank Laubach, *Channels of Spiritual Power* (Westwood, Nj: Fleming H. Revell, 1954), 54. Italics in the original.
2. Laubach, *Channels of Spiritual Power*, 55–56.
3. In Frank Laubach's *Channels of Spiritual Power*, chapters 5–7 contain a marvelous discussion of these blockages and how to break them.
4. Frank Laubach, *Channels of Spiritual Power*, 71–72.
5. Watchman Nee, *The Joyful Heart* (Fort Washington, PA: CLC Publications, 1977), 76.

LAW 35: STAY FAITHFUL TO YOUR CALLING

1. Ephesians 6:13, NKJV.
2. Frank Viola, *Finding Organic Church* (Colorado Springs: David C. Cook, 2009), 166.
3. Watchman Nee, *The Normal Christian Church Life* (Anaheim, CA: Living Stream Ministry, 1980), 17.

LAW 36: DO NOT GO BEYOND YOUR GIFT

1. For details, see my article "Rethinking the Five-Fold Ministry" at frankviola .org/rethinking-the-five-fold-ministry.
2. I don't have time or space to flesh this principle out here, but I've addressed it in detail in *From Eternity to Here*. The third part of the book shows how Christ sees His body.

LAW 37: BE QUICK TO APOLOGIZE

1. Remember Law 1 (Never Hurt God's People).
2. Mario Batali, quoted in Jason Hanna, "Mario Batali Includes Recipe with Apology for 'Past Behavior,'" *CNN Entertainment*, December 18, 2017.
3. Mario Cuomo, quoted in Michael Scherer and Josh Dawsey, "New York Gov. Andrew M. Cuomo Says He Will Not Resign, Offers New Apology for His Behavior with Women," *Washington Post*, March 3, 2021.

LAW 38: WATCH YOUR VOCABULARY

1. For details on this topic, check out episode #10 of the Insurgence podcast, "Profanity, Swearing, Cursing, and the Kingdom of God."
2. Karl Barth, *Theologische Fragen und Antworten* (1957), 183–184, quoted in R. J. Erler and R. Marquard, eds., *A Karl Barth Reader*, trans. G. W. Bromiley (Grand Rapids: Eerdmans, 1986), 8–9.

3. James D. G. Dunn, *New Testament Theology in Dialogue* (Philadelphia: Westminster Press, 1987), 126–129. In my book *Pagan Christianity?*, I show historically that the clergy-laity concept and vocabulary is unscriptural.
4. See chapters 2–3 in *Revise Us Again: Living from a Revised Christian Script* (Colorado Springs: David C. Cook, 2010).

LAW 39: DO NOT DEFEND YOURSELF
1. See Matthew 26:63; 27:12, 14; Mark 14:61; 15:5; Luke 23:9; John 19:9; Isaiah 53:7; Acts 8:32.
2. Bob Laurent, *Watchman Nee: Man of Suffering* (Uhrichsville, OH: Barbour, 1998), quoted in chapter 1, "Family Background."
3. A. W. Tozer, *Born After Midnight* (Camp Hill, PA: WingSpread Publishers, 2008), 117.

LAW 40: REMAIN POOR IN SPIRIT
1. The leaders in Jerusalem were experts in the Scriptures.
2. Kenneth Bailey, *Jesus Through Middle Eastern Eyes* (Downers Grove, IL: IVP Academic, 2008), 69.
3. The ASV and ERV also use the word *poor* in this passage to refer to a person's spirit.
4. Leonard Sweet and Frank Viola, *Jesus Speaks: Learning to Recognize and Respond to the Lord's Voice* (Nashville: Thomas Nelson, 2016), 99.
5. Sweet and Viola, *Jesus Speaks*, 99–100.

LAW 41: RETHINK SUCCESS
1. See 1 Samuel 17 for a vivid example.
2. I wrote about nonnegotiable values in chapter 39 of *Hang On, Let Go.*

LAW 43: SPEAK TO THE HEART
1. For a list of verses that discuss the human spirit, see Proverbs 20:27; Luke 23:46; Acts 7:59; Romans 1:19; 8:16; 1 Corinthians 2:11; 1 Thessalonians 5:23; Hebrews 4:12; James 2:26. Throughout Scripture, the heart is sometimes a reference to the mind, the emotions, or the will. Other times it's a reference to the conscience, which is part of the human spirit.
2. See Coda V, "A Nicodemus Moment," where I elaborate this point.
3. Some were also saying "I'm of Christ." These believers were claiming that they were following Jesus, that they were "the church of Christ" while everyone else in the ekklesia wasn't. Paul included them in the divisive groups. The same sectarian spirit was also driving those who were claiming they were "of Paul."

LAW 44: NEVER WASTE A TRIAL
1. See Appendix 1 in *Hang On, Let Go*, "Who Brought Your Trial?"
2. Watchman Nee, *From Faith to Faith* (Christian Fellowship Publishers, New York, 1984), 61–62, 75. In *God's Work,* Nee discusses how brokenness releases

God's life (Watchman Nee, *God's Work,* Christian Fellowship Publishers, New York, 1974), 23–26.

3. T. Austin-Sparks, *Daily Open Windows: Excerpts from the Messages of T. Austin-Sparks,* ebook, April 10.
4. A. W. Tozer, *Man: The Dwelling Place of God* (Harrisburg, PA: Christian Publications, 1966), 101.
5. David Wilkerson, "The Making of a Man of God," WorldChallenge.org, February 1, 2010.
6. Frank Viola, *Hang On, Let Go* (Carol Stream, IL: Tyndale Momentum, 2021).

LAW 45: AVOID TOXIC PEOPLE

1. Just look at the kinds of people who were attracted to Jesus in the Gospels. And who joined David at the cave of Adullam (1 Samuel 22:1-2).
2. Letters of commendation are mentioned and/or exemplified in Acts 13:3-4; 14:26; 15:2-4, 22, 25-27; 18:27; Romans 16:1-2; 1 Corinthians 4:17; 16:3, 10-11, 15-18; 2 Corinthians 3:1; 8:16-24; Ephesians 6:21-22; Philippians 2:19-30; 4:2-3; Colossians 4:7-10; 1 Thessalonians 3:2; 5:12-13; 3 John 1:5-8.

LAW 48: REALIZE IT DOESN'T WORK

1. Those books are *Pagan Christianity?*, *Reimagining Church*, and *Finding Organic Church*.
2. Ironically, the New Testament doesn't know anything about an "individual Christian existence." On the contrary, the Christian life is intensely corporate. It's meant to be lived in community. See *Reimagining Church* for details.

CODA I: THE DANGER OF GOD'S POWER

1. For examples, see 1 Samuel 4:21; 16:14-23; Judges 16:19-20.
2. C. S. Lewis, *The Lion, the Witch, and the Wardrobe* (New York: HarperCollins, 1950), 182.
3. There are a few exceptions, but saying "tell no one" was His standard practice.
4. Interestingly, a person can be exposed to God's miraculous power and remain untransformed (see Luke 16:31).

CODA III: WHEN CHRISTIAN LEADERS DENY THE FAITH

1. Talis Shelbourne, "Jon Steingard, Lead Singer of Christian Band Hawk Nelson, Announces He Has Stopped Believing in God," Heavy.com, May 26, 2020.
2. For my treatment of what organic church life is, see *Reimagining Church* and my numerous blog articles at frankviola.org/category/church.

CODA V: A NICODEMUS MOMENT

1. T. Austin-Sparks, "The Voice of the Son of God," *A Witness and a Testimony* magazine, May–June 1946, vol. 24–3.

ABOUT THE AUTHOR

Frank Viola has helped thousands of people around the world deepen their relationship with Jesus Christ and enter into a more vibrant and authentic experience of church. His mission is to help serious followers of Jesus know their Lord more deeply so they can experience real transformation and make a lasting impact. Viola has written many books on these themes, including *God's Favorite Place on Earth*, *From Eternity to Here*, and his landmark book, *Insurgence: Reclaiming the Gospel of the Kingdom*. His blog, *Beyond Evangelical*, is rated as one of the most popular in Christian circles today. Visit his website at frankviola.org.